# Garden
# Birds

Stephen Moss

HarperCollins*Publishers* Ltd.
77-85 Fulham Palace Road
London
W6 8JB

The Collins website address is:
www.collins.co.uk

Collins is a registered trademark of
HarperCollinsPublishers Ltd.

First published in 2005

10 09 08 07 06 05

10 9 8 7 6 5 4 3 2 1

A catalogue record for this book is available from the British Library.

ISBN 0 00 717789 5

Designed by Penny Dawes

Colour reproduction by Colourscan, Singapore
Printed and bound by Printing Express Ltd, Hong Kong

# CONTENTS

**Part One**

Introduction                                    5

Watching Garden Birds                          6

Feeding                                        10

Planting for birds                             17

Nest sites                                     22

Water                                          28

Pests and predators                            32

Towns and parks and their birds                36


**Part Two**

Grebes                                         40

Cormorants                                     44

Herons and Storks                              46

Swans, Geese and Ducks                         50

Birds of Prey                                  74

Game Birds                                     82

Rails                                          84

Gulls and Terns                                88

Pigeons and Doves                              98

Parakeets                                     106

Owls                                          108

Swifts                                        110

Kingfisher and Hoopoe                         112

Woodpeckers                          116
Larks                                124
Swallows and Martins                 128
Pipits                               134
Wagtails                             136
Waxwing                              142
Wren and Dunnock                     144
Thrushes and Chats                   148
Warblers                             164
Flycatchers                          178
Tits                                 180
Nuthatch and Treecreepers            190
Orioles                              196
Crows                                198
Starlings                            208
Sparrows                             210
Finches                              212
Buntings                             232

Next steps                           236
Index                                237

# INTRODUCTION

Helping garden birds, by providing food, water and places to roost and nest, is one of the most popular pastimes in Britain: roughly two out of every three of us do it on a regular basis. Of course the primary reason we do so is to help the birds themselves: without our assistance millions would die every year. But though praiseworthy, a selfless concern for our fellow creatures is not the only motive. We also do it because it brings us pleasure. Indeed, the constant comings and goings of birds right outside your kitchen or sitting room window is one of the best ways of getting close to nature.

   This book includes the species most typically found in British and European gardens, parks and towns. Some, like the House Sparrow and Blue Tit, are familiar garden visitors; others, such as the Mallard and Tufted Duck, are more likely to be seen in areas such as your local park.

   I hope that you find this a useful and interesting book, which will enable you to get pleasure from the birds in your local area, and learn more about their lives.

# WATCHING GARDEN BIRDS

As we are at last beginning to realise, getting close to nature is good for us. It now appears that regular contact with wild nature, in any form, is good for our health. We've always known that hiking across the moors and mountain tops makes us feel physically better; but now we are starting to understand the benefits to our mental health as well. Put simply, taking a close interest in living creatures does us good – and maybe even helps us to live longer!

If you are going to get close to nature, what better way to begin than with the living creatures in your own garden? Of these, birds are both the most visible and the easiest to identify, so they are the best place to start. Later on, you may find yourself converted to the whole idea of giving over part of your garden for wildlife – of making space for nature alongside you and your family. You might put out a small mammal table; make a compost heap, rockery or woodpile to attract insects and frogs; even plant a hay meadow. But for now, why not start with the simplest and most basic way to attract wildlife: putting out some food and water for the birds. You'll soon become hooked, and may even start down the road to becoming a fully-fledged birdwatcher. If you do,

then take a look around your local park, or visit a nearby nature reserve, gravel pit or woodland, where you will find a wider range of species.

Britain's gardens cover an area estimated at between one and three million acres – whatever the true size, this represents Britain's most important natural resource – making them our biggest nature reserve. Small changes made by everyone who owns a garden really can make a difference, and nowadays, with so many of our once common species in trouble, that difference is truly vital. When birds like the Song Thrush, Starling and House Sparrow start to disappear from areas where they were once common and widespread, there is something serious happening. But by providing the right things to attract these birds into your garden you will be creating a welcome oasis where they can survive and thrive. Hopefully as those in power begin to realise the worth of our common birds, policies in areas such as agriculture and land use will shift towards a more environmentally friendly approach. In the meantime, we can do our bit by making our garden into a little nature reserve.

Not that it's all bad news for our garden birds. Some species are doing rather well: Robins, Wrens and Blue Tits in particular seem to be thriving, while once scarce garden visitors such as the Siskin, Goldfinch and Blackcap are becoming more and more regular visitors. Of course the range of species you see will depend on many different factors: whether you live in a town, suburb or a village; whether you live in the north or south of Britain; and the size and shape of your garden and its contents. But the things you need to do to attract a greater variety of species into your garden are more or less the same. They basically boil down to providing a regular supply of high energy food; clean, fresh water so the birds can drink and bathe; trees, bushes and shrubs for them to shelter, roost and build their nests; and a safe environment where predators cannot easily attack them.

Before you start, it's worth making one simple investment. By getting a decent pair of binoculars you will enjoy the birds in your garden much more. You don't need to pay a fortune, though it's worth spending a little more to get a better model if you can. Looking at birds through binoculars opens up a whole new world of delight and fascination: even the humble Blue Tit or Blackbird look fabulous when you get a really close up view. And it will help you identify more unusual visitors to your garden, using the illustrations in part two of this book to help you.

Finally, you may be put off by the idea that all this is too much hard work; or perhaps by the cost or the time involved. Rest assured, creating a more bird-friendly environment really doesn't take that much effort, and the rewards will be more or less instantaneous. So have a go!

*Wild Guide Garden Birds* is divided into two main parts. Part one covers all the different things you need to do to attract birds into your garden, including sections on: feeding, planting for birds, nest sites, water, pests and predators, changes to garden birds and town and park birds. Don't feel you have to do everything at once: you can start by putting out some food and water; then gradually extend your scope by doing some planting or putting up a nestbox or two. Whatever you do really will make a difference!

Part two includes the species most typically found in British and European gardens, parks and towns. Some, like the Robin, are residents, (they breed and live here all year round), while others, such as the Swallow and House Martin, are purely summer visitors. A few species, such as the White Stork, Serin and Golden Oriole, are rare in Britain but fairly regular town and garden visitors on the Continent.

The calendar for each species shows when you are likely to see it, with shaded areas indicating when it is present in the UK. The maps show the distribution for each species throughout Europe. Green indicates the bird is resident, blue indicates it is a winter visitor only, and yellow indicates it is a summer visitor. Brown shows the breeding range, abandoned in winter. The ID fact file for each species is a quick way of checking its size, voice, and feeding habits, as well as any lookalikes that you might mistake it for.

# FEEDING

The first question people often ask is why should we feed garden birds at all? Can't they find food for themselves? In fact one of the problems faced by birds today is that we have changed their natural habitats so much that although in some places there is a surplus of natural food, in others there is a dearth.

For example, farming used to be in tune with nature, and wild creatures were able to coexist with farmers. After the Second World War, however, there was a drive towards increased food production above all else, and the wildlife came a poor third behind crop yield and profits. As a result many former farmland species now find it a struggle to survive, and are increasingly coming into urban and suburban areas in order to find food.

Likewise many other ancient habitats such as hedgerows and hay meadows, which although man-made still supported a wide variety of birds and other wildlife, have declined almost to the point of disappearing entirely from the face of our landscape.

So the reason we should feed garden birds is quite simply because we have a moral duty to do so. Another good reason is because it works: the more you feed, and the greater variety of food you provide, the more species will take advantage of this.

Finally, by watching the behaviour of birds visiting your bird table or feeders you will learn a huge amount about their lives; and hopefully be encouraged to take a greater interest in their conservation. Here are a few things that might surprise you:

■ If you see a maximum of ten Blue Tits or Great Tits on your feeders, you can calculate that there are over 100 individual birds visiting your garden in the course of a single day!

■ Birds do a feeding circuit, flitting between gardens to maximise their chances of finding food – which is why at certain times of day they seem to disappear completely. In winter, a small bird needs to eat about one quarter of its body weight every day simply in order to survive.

■ If you see or hear a Blackcap in your garden between March and September it is probably a local breeding bird, which will fly off to spend the winter in Spain of North Africa. But if you see one feeding from October to February it will be an immigrant bird which breeds in central Europe.

■ In winter, look out for Redwings and Fieldfares, two thrushes which although they only breed rarely in Britain, winter here in their millions. They come here from their breeding grounds in Scandinavia and northern Russia to take advantage of our mild winter climate and plenty of free food.

## Before you start

When you start feeding garden birds there are a few things you need to remember:

■ If you do decide to feed the birds in your garden, you mustn't suddenly stop doing so, as by then the birds will have become dependent on you.
■ You don't need to provide a huge feeding station straight away. A simple bird table is fine, or even one or two peanut or seed feeders.
■ You can now feed all year round. It used to be assumed that garden birds didn't need feeding during the spring and summer months, but we now know that when they have young in the nest is a critical time, when the adults may starve.
■ Finally, don't forget that birds need water too! (See pages 28-31.)

## Food and feeding requirements

Don't forget that different species have different food and feeding requirements. These broadly break down into five categories:

**Peanuts and seeds in feeders:** traditionally, we have always fed peanuts to birds; at first in string mesh feeders, later in more sturdy and rigid metal ones, which at least give some protection from attack by squirrels. Peanuts are still a staple diet for many species, especially Blue and Great Tits, Greenfinches and House Sparrows. However, increasingly it seems that peanuts are not as preferable as some alternatives, especially high-energy sunflower seeds. Where both peanuts and seeds are provided side by side, most birds go for the seeds every time – mainly because they are much more rich in energy which means they can feed for a shorter time and still get the nutrition they need. So if you have only provided nuts so far, why not have a go with either black sunflower seeds, or even better, sunflower hearts (which have already been shelled and therefore do not make any mess). These are more expensive then peanuts or an ordinary seed mix, but much less wasteful and better for the birds.

**Food on bird tables:** this has always been the easiest way to put out food for the birds, and remains an excellent method of attracting species that either cannot feed on seed and peanut feeders, or are reluctant to. The first category includes larger birds such as Wood Pigeons and Collared Doves; the second category birds like Robins, which although they will hang onto a wire mesh feeder often prefer to feed standing up! Foods to put out include kitchen scraps, bread, fruit (dried or fresh), grated cheese, cooked rice, cooked vegetables, and even pet food.

**Food on the ground:** inevitably if you have a bird table or feeders some food gets spilt onto the ground, where it provides a free meal for birds such as House Sparrows. But some birds such as thrushes and Blackbirds prefer feeding on the ground, so you can put out windfall apples, especially in autumn.

**Live food:** some species love live food – after all it is part of their natural diet for all insect eaters. The simplest way to provide it is by putting mealworms or waxworms into a smooth sided bowl, or a specialised 'mealworm feeder' available from several mail order outlets. This should attract Robins, and also Jays.

**Specialised foods:** other specialised foods include fat bars (great for Robins, Long-tailed Tits and wintering Blackcaps), and a tiny form of sunflower seed known as nyger, which is perfect for Goldfinches, as they are the only species with a delicate enough bill to break the seeds open to get inside.

# Where to put your feeders

Where you put your feeders is almost as important as what you put inside them! But if you follow these two simple rules you should be okay:

■ A bird table should be mounted either on a strong and sturdy pole fixed into the ground, or free standing on its own base if provided. Alternatives, especially if you are pushed for space, include hanging the table from a mount fixed to a tree, wall or fence – but be careful that this doesn't put it within easy reach of predators such as cats. Ideally it should be about head height, so you can see what is going on.

■ Bird feeders should be hung from a tree or a mount fixed to a fence or wall, or on a freestanding pole (which may deter predators). Don't put a free standing feeder too far out into your lawn as the birds may be put off – some like to perch on a nearby branch or twig before coming in to feed.

## Going further

There are several reputable bird food and feeder dealers who deliver straight to your door, and maintain the highest standards of product. They may be slightly more expensive than your local market stall or pet shop, but the standard of the products is much higher. Check out the following:

**Haith's:** 0800 298 7054 or www.haiths.com
**CJ Wildbird Foods:** 0800 731 2820 or www.birdfood.co.uk
**RSPB Shop:** 0870 606 6333 or www.rspbshop.co.uk

There are also two surveys in which you can participate: one all year round, the other for just one hour every year. The RSPB's 'Big Garden Birdwatch' takes place one weekend in January, and all you have to do is to list the number of species actually visiting (rather than flying over) your garden for one hour over a particular weekend. For more details contact the RSPB on 01767 680551, or www.rspb.org.uk.

If you are really keen to help, then the BTO's 'Garden Bird Watch' is a year round monitoring project, in which you fill in regular weekly details of which birds come to feed in your garden. The scheme now has more than 16,000 participants and is a really useful way for scientists to get to understand changes in the populations and distribution of our garden birds. Contact the BTO on 01842 750050 or www.bto.org.

# PLANTING FOR BIRDS

When you decide which plants to put into your garden you are spoilt for choice. Even if you have decided that you prefer to plant wildlife-friendly ones then the range is huge. And making space for nature in your garden doesn't mean turning it into an unkempt wilderness; all you need to do is to consider wildlife when you are choosing what to plant.

The key is to provide a good selection of different plants chosen for different purposes, such as nectar-producing flowers to attract insects, berry-bearing plants to provide food in autumn and winter, and a range of plants which will provide places to roost, shelter and nest at different times of the year and for different species.

However large or small your garden, it is important that you try to provide a good cross-section of plants in the following categories:

**Seed-bearing plants** such as teasel and sunflower, to attract finches, sparrows and buntings, especially during the late summer and autumn.

**Flowering plants** such as annual and perennial wildflowers, which attract insects including butterflies which in turn produce caterpillars, a vital food resource for young birds during the breeding season.

**Climbing plants** such as honeysuckle, clematis and various kinds of ivy, which provide a combination of food for insects and birds and a place for species such as Blackbirds and Song Thrushes to build their nest.

**Berry-bearing plants** such as holly, cotoneaster and brambles, which provide high-energy food during late summer, autumn and winter for warblers and thrushes.

If your garden is big enough, larger fruiting trees such as apple or oak, which support a variety of insect life, as well as providing fruit for a wide range of species.

When planning your garden try also to provide different plants at different levels, as some species such as the Wren and Dunnock prefer to stay close to the ground for much of the time, while others such as Mistle Thrush or Blackbird are more often found perched high on a bush or tree. The same applies to nesting birds, with different species nesting either close to the ground, at eye level or high in the foliage.

# Native plants

It's often said that you should always try to plant native flowers and other plants in your garden rather than exotic species. Although it is true that by and large native plants will attract a greater variety of wild creatures, it is not a strict rule: for example, buddleia, an exotic import, is marvellous for attracting butterflies during mid to late summer. But if you have a choice between a native or non-native variety of the same plant, then by and large the native one will support a wide range of insects and other invertebrates, which makes it a better choice for the birds.

If you have the space, then the plants most likely to attract a really wide range of birds are large trees such as oak or beech. However, most gardens are too small, though if you live in a rural area you may be lucky enough to have large trees either in or backing onto your garden. If you do, then make sure you keep them! A more practical choice for most people is smaller trees such as willow and alder, both of which attract a wide range of birds, with alder cones especially popular amongst our two smaller finches, Redpoll and Siskin. Fruit trees such as crab apple and even apple are much easier and quicker to grow, and provide fruit in

autumn as well as attracting insects in spring and summer. Even easier and quicker to grow are hedgerow plants such as hawthorn and elder: these not only provide flowers to attract a wide range of insects in spring and early summer, but also have berries in late summer and autumn, which are excellent food for thrushes and migrant warblers such as Whitethroat and Blackcap. These large plants also provide plenty of nesting cover.

If you have a smaller garden, especially one which doesn't get much sun, then why not consider climbing plants such as ivy. These grow quickly and are excellent places for species such as Wrens to build their nest; they also provide berries during the winter. Honeysuckle is also a great garden plant, with fragrant flowers and berries too.

Finally, flowering plants, including annual ones such as poppies and cornflowers, and perennials such as cowslip, are particularly good for attracting butterflies, which in turn lay eggs which hatch into caterpillars – more food for hungry baby birds! And if you don't mind a slightly messier area at the back of your garden, stinging nettles and brambles will provide an excellent food resource for all kinds of wildlife.

## Non-native plants

Although it is generally best to plant native species such as those already mentioned, don't overlook non-native varieties: they may not be quite so politically correct but they often look very attractive and provide useful resources such as food and shelter for our garden birds. Seed-bearing plants such as Sunflower provide a useful late summer and autumn resource for seed-eating species such as finches and buntings, while the buds of flowering plants such as Forsythia are also very popular, especially with Bullfinches.

But if you want to attract a range of birds into your garden, and provide much needed food during late autumn and winter, then you need to plant a range of berry-bearing shrubs and bushes. Start off with well-known garden plants such as Pyracantha and Cotoneaster, which provides a regular supply of bright red berries, especially popular with winter thrushes such as Fieldfare and Redwing, and resident species such as the Mistle Thrush.

Finally, don't overlook one of the least popular garden plants of all: the infamous Leylandii cypress. These have been the subject of many a neighbourhood dispute, as they have a habit of growing very rapidly and can easily block out the light in a very short time. However, their dense foliage is very appealing to many garden birds, including House Sparrow, Greenfinch and Collared Dove, as a safe place to nest and roost. The tiny Goldcrest also likes to nest deep inside the dark green foliage.

For more advice on planting for birds, check out the following:

**Royal Horticultural Society:** www.rhs.org.uk
**RSPB**, which provides free leaflets on the subject: 01767 680551, or www.rspb.org.uk
**CJ Wildbird Foods**, whose *Handbook of Garden Feeding* has some useful products: 0800 731 2820 or www.birdfood.co.uk

# NEST SITES

As well as providing food for birds, which will help them survive the rigours of harsh winter weather, it's also a good idea to provide places for them to nest and raise their family. In recent years this has become even more vital, as many natural habitats are fast disappearing and there are fewer places in which some species can nest.

So your job is to provide a selection of nest sites: some natural, such as climbing plants and shrubs; others artificial, such as nestboxes. By creating various niches where the birds can decide to nest you will help maintain healthy breeding populations, especially important for species such as the Starling, Song Thrush and House Sparrow, which appear to be in a major decline.

## Plants to attract nesting birds

If you have a large rural garden then you probably already have lots of suitable places for birds to build their nest, and indeed lots of different birds nesting each spring. But what

if your garden is smaller, and in a less promising location? In fact even the smallest urban garden will attract some birds, while if you live in the suburbs, you may be amazed at just how many different bird may come to your garden to breed.

Garden shrubs such as berberis, and climbers such as honeysuckle and clematis, are ideal for nesting birds, as they provide dense cover in a safe place. Ivy is also great for nesting Wrens, while the larger evergreens such as cypresses have plenty of dark places for birds such as House Sparrows or Greenfinches to hide their nest away from prying eyes. And any hedgerow plant, especially hawthorn and elder, are not only an attractive addition to your garden foliage but also much loved by many nesting birds. And once again, if you have larger trees either in or just outside your garden make sure you take care of them and that they are not felled; they are fabulous places for all sorts of birds including hole-nesting tits and woodpeckers.

## Nestboxes

Probably the most important invention to help garden birds was when the German Baron von Berlepsch first created a small wooden box with an entrance hole in order to persuade hole-nesting birds such as tits to breed in it. That was back in the late 19th century, since when nestboxes have become an integral part of any bird-friendly garden.

The principle of a nestbox is simple: at a time when natural holes and crevices are harder and harder to find, thanks to the felling of trees and the cutting down of any dead or dying specimens, they provide a quick and easy alternative for birds to breed.

Nestboxes have several advantages over natural nest sites: they are in gardens, near to the best food supply; they are clean and well-sited (at least they should be!); and they are often better at keeping out predators. For us they have an added bonus: they enable us to get great views of nesting birds right outside our back window. And by taking careful note of the birds' comings and goings, and the timing of their nesting attempts, we may also contribute to scientific knowledge of our breeding birds.

# Choosing a nestbox

Nowadays, when it comes to buying a nestbox you are spoilt for choice. There are crevice shaped ones for Treecreepers, huge ones for Barn Owls and Kestrels, and cup-shaped ones for House Martins. But most people start with one of the two basic varieties:

The 'tit box': a standard rectangular box with a small hole in the front at the top, so that the parent birds can get in and out to brood and feed the young chicks. A 25mm diameter hole will suit Blue Tits, while Great Tits need a slightly larger one of 28mm diameter, and House Sparrows require an even larger one of 32mm diameter.

The open-fronted box: basically the same design as the tit box but with a large rectangular entrance at the front, which allows species such as Robin or Pied Wagtail to nest. If you are really lucky, your open-fronted box may even attract a Spotted Flycatcher, though this summer visitor is becoming increasingly rare in recent years.

When you are buying a nestbox, you should really try to avoid the fancy designs such as those often sold as ornaments in garden centres. As far as nesting birds are concerned, form and function are much more important

than style: in essence, the simpler a box design the better for the birds themselves. So buy your nestbox from a reputable source such as the RSPB or one of the leading bird food suppliers.

You can make your own nestboxes, though to be honest it isn't really worth it unless you plan to do so in bulk – say a dozen or more boxes at a time. For further information you can get a free leaflet containing plans from the RSPB www.rspb.org.uk or if you want to explore more ambitious designs for more unusual species, then the BTO provide an excellent guide, *Nestboxes*, by Chris de Feu (www.bto.org).

## Siting a nestbox

Once you have bought, been given or made your nestbox, the most important decision is exactly where to put it. Badly sited nestboxes will either be ignored by your local birds, or worse still, an inexperienced pair will attempt to nest and suffer from overheating or attention from predators. So follow these basic rules, and you should be successful:

■ Try to put up your nestbox during the late autumn or early winter, after the end of the previous breeding season, to give the birds the chance to get used to it.

■ Fix the box on a sturdy and solid back, such as a garden fence, wall or post; ideally between one and a half metres and five metres above the ground.

■ Avoid putting the box where it will get direct sunlight during the hottest part of the day: i.e. facing between south and west. In practice, it's best to position the box so that the entrance hole faces any direction from north-east and south-east, or if that is not possible, in an area well shaded by foliage.

■ Try to strike a balance between a site to which the birds can gain easy access, using suitable perches; and one that predators such as cats cannot reach. This may not always be easy, but if in doubt it is better to have no nestbox at all than one that a cat may get to.

■ Once the box is in place, please resist the understandable temptation to inspect the box constantly, as this is likely to disturb the nesting birds and make them desert. If you do wish to inspect the box (for example if you are participating in the BTO's excellent Nest Record Scheme), then follow the BTO's Code of Conduct (www.bto.org).

■ After the end of the breeding season, from September or October onwards, you should open the box, remove any remaining nesting material, unhatched eggs or dead young (use rubber gloves for hygiene or if you are squeamish), and give the box a thorough clean with boiling water.

Never use strong household chemicals such as bleach, as these may linger and cause harm to the birds the next year. The best time to clean your nestbox is between October and December.

## Care of baby birds

What should you do if you find a baby bird that appears to have fallen out of its nest? Surprisingly perhaps, the usual answer is 'nothing at all'. Baby birds often leave the nest a day or two before they are able to fly, and are looked after by the parents, which will bring food and try to make sure that the baby stays in a safe place, out of sight of marauding predators. With luck after a day or two the chick can feed and fly on its own.

Occasionally a tiny chick does fall out of its nest far earlier than it should, and is obviously incapable of surviving. If you can find the nest, try to put the chick back as soon as possible, though if it has been exposed to the elements for a while it is unlikely to survive. If you do take any chick indoors it is likely to die, which may be distressing as well as counter-productive. But do remember that the vast majority of baby birds do die before they reach maturity: this is Nature's way of keeping populations in check. So while it may be upsetting, console yourself with the thought that what you are witnessing is part of the natural cycle.

# WATER

Next to providing food and somewhere to nest, water is the single most important factor in terms of attracting birds to your garden, and helping them to survive. By providing a good, regular supply of clean water you will allow birds to perform two vital daily functions: drinking and bathing. You can do so either the easy way – by putting out water in a bird bath – or if you are a bit more ambitious, you can also construct a garden pond. This will not only attract birds and provide an opportunity for them to drink and bathe, but will also attract a wide range of other garden wildlife from foxes to frogs and dragonflies to grass snakes.

Drinking water is particularly important, especially during hot summer days or prolonged periods of drought, which seem to be getting more and more regular nowadays. Although birds do not need to drink as frequently as we do, most do need to drink at least once a day – more if they are seed-eating species such as finches or sparrows (insect eating species do manage to get a considerable portion of their daily water requirements from their food). Unfortunately, drinking is one of the most dangerous activities for any small bird, as they are very vulnerable to attack by predators such as cats or Sparrowhawks at this time. This is why many birds drink quickly and furtively, grabbing quick sips as they do so, and flying off at the least sign of danger.

Birds also need to bathe regularly, as if they fail to do so then their plumage may become matted, and they will be more vulnerable to disease. Clean plumage is also a much better defence against cold weather, as it allows birds to fluff up their feathers, trapping a layer of air as a defence again the cold. After bathing many birds sit for a while and preen their feathers, systematically running their beak along the shaft in order to tidy up their plumage. In warm weather they may also sit in a sunny corner of your garden to dry out their feathers.

Most birds bathe once or twice a day, either in the morning or evening. So by providing a regular source of clean, fresh water, you can save the birds the time and

trouble of seeking out a nearby pond or puddle. During the winter, when they need to feed almost all the time, this really can make a difference to their chances of survival.

## Bird baths

When it comes to bird baths, you have two options: either buy a ready made model, or make your own out of a suitable shallow dish or container. But whatever you do, follow some basic rules:

■ Try to avoid fancy designs sold in garden centres, as they may be unsuitable, especially for smaller birds, which require a well-designed bath. They are also often garishly coloured which may put the birds off.

■ The ideal bird bath is sturdy and solid, with shallow and deep parts, which allow different species of birds to drink and bathe at the same time.

■ Avoid too smooth a surface, as the birds' feet may slip on it. For this reason glass bowls are not really suitable.

■ Make sure you refill the bird bath with clean, fresh tap water once a day.

■ Pay particular attention to hygiene, especially during hot, dry weather in summer, when bacteria can build up very rapidly, spreading disease amongst birds.

## Garden ponds

If you really want to provide a five star service for your garden birds, and indeed for many other kinds of wildlife, then you can do no better thing than build a garden pond. Even if you have a very small garden there is usually a small space where you can provide some kind of a water feature, and in a larger garden the sky's the limit! Garden ponds are also a lovely feature for you, providing a real focal point to your garden.

Ponds are good for birds in all sorts of ways. First, they provide a quick, convenient alternative to the local pond or puddle – assuming there is one. With the decline in farm ponds during the past few years garden ponds are even more important nowadays. Second, they greatly increase the range of insects that are attracted to your garden, helping to broaden the food resource for your garden birds. They're also great places for all kinds of other creatures such as frogs, toads and newts.

# Planning and constructing a garden pond

Although making a garden pond may seem difficult, there are various guides on the market, which provide step-by-step instructions on how to do so. The key things to remember are:

**Siting:** make sure you put the pond in the right place, ideally at the lowest point of your garden and in an area that receives plenty of sunlight. Try to avoid putting the pond directly beneath large trees, as falling leaves may cause problems.

**Equipment:** make sure you have everything you need (including suitable tools).

**Planning:** pay attention to the shape and size of your pond. Take your time to decide how big a pond you want, and the exact shape – you won't be able to change it later on!

**Planting:** stock your pond with a selection of native water plants, using species which provide submerged and floating vegetation, as well as those which grow around the edge of the pond.

**Water:** 'borrow' a bucketful of water from an established pond, as this will contain all the useful microscopic life you need. But make sure you avoid transplanting alien invaders such as Canadian pondweed.

## Pond maintenance and safety

During hot weather or prolonged periods of drought make sure you regularly clear algae off the surface of the pond, and top up the water level if it starts to fall considerably. In autumn remove fallen leaves as they may also make the pond stagnant, and in winter weather break the ice so that the birds can still get to the water.

If you have small children, prevent them from getting access to your pond by putting on a strong cover which cannot be moved. Every year several children drown in garden ponds. Make sure such a tragedy doesn't happen in yours.

# PESTS AND PREDATORS

When you have put so much effort into making your garden good for birds it can be really demoralising when the pests and predators move in too. But in a way this is hardly surprising – by creating such a great place for birds to feed, drink and nest, you have also created a free lunch for a whole range of other animals. So don't be too disappointed: there are still things you can do to fend them off!

The various pests and predators fall into two main categories: those you feel able to tolerate, and those with whom you want to fight an all-out war. Depending on your opinion, the former category may include Grey Squirrels (after all, their antics are fairly amusing), Sparrowhawks (which at least have the advantage of being wild predators), and perhaps Wood Mice, which are a perfectly harmless creature who happens to take advantage of a free food supply. Those which most garden owners regard as beyond the pale include Magpies, Brown Rats, and especially my own personal bugbear, the domestic cat.

There are several things you can do to discourage these unwelcome visitors, or at least to reduce their effectiveness, but you must admit to yourself from the very start that your

garden is unlikely to be a pest and predator-free zone, so learning to minimise the damage and adopt at least a degree of tolerance is probably the best course of action.

In the end, you can also comfort yourself with the thought that the more of these creatures attracted to your garden, the better job you must be doing at creating a wildlife friendly environment. After all, they wouldn't be there if there was nothing to eat, would they!

## Predators

It is only natural that some creatures should prey on others, and the bird world is no exception to the rule. Large birds such as Magpies, Jays and Sparrowhawks feed themselves and their young on small birds (and in the case of the first two, on eggs), and this inevitably means loss of life for some songbirds. Although it can be upsetting, you should console yourself with the thought that at least their presence in your garden is part of nature's rich tapestry. Despite newspaper headlines and a long-running campaign to depict them as evil killers, these predators do not have any lasting effect on bird populations. Unfortunately, a rise in the populations of these three species has coincided with a fall in the numbers of some of our favourite garden birds, causing some people to put two and two together and make five.

The creature that does have a very harmful effect on our garden birds (and indeed on small mammals too) is the domestic cat. The problem is that cats are not part of the natural food chain, and are given a helping hand by being fed by us. We also keep them at unnaturally high densities, up to 500 times what would be found in a normal predator-prey situation. It is never pleasant to see the victims of cats, as they often fail to kill a bird or small mammal and deposit it on your kitchen floor as if asking you to do so! It has been reliably estimated that Britain's seven million cats kill anything between 28 and 75 million birds every single year. Many of these are adult birds, which in the longer term is likely to prove harmful to bird populations.

Few people would argue against any way of reducing the death toll from cat predation. One simple way to do this is to make sure your cat wears a bell, which is supposed to warn birds of its approach. Another approach, if your neighbour's cat comes into your garden, is to install a cat deterrent. These machines emit a high-pitched sound inaudible to the human ear but intolerable to cats.

## Pests

The whole notion of a 'pest' is a subjective one, with some people's 'pest' being another's favourite garden visitor. Squirrels are one such example: many people do everything they possibly can to keep them out of the garden, while others take a more tolerant view; a few even building complicated 'assault courses' to test the animal's ingenuity.

Many people also have a problem with rats and mice, but in fact these do not cause too many problems, and a 'live and let live' view should be adopted if you can. If they are causing a major problem then you can always resort to humane pest controllers.

Most gardeners also spend much of their time in a battle against insect and other invertebrate pests, such as snails, slugs and caterpillars. If they become a real problem then there are wildlife-friendly methods such as beer traps for slugs, but again the natural course is the best – encourage Song Thrushes and your slug problem will go away!

## Other hazards

Pests and predators are not the only hazards facing birds in your garden: there are several other potential dangers, which you should do your best to help the birds avoid.

**Glass windows and doors:** many people are distressed to discover a small bird, or worse still a large predator such as a Sparrowhawk, lying dead beside a large window or glass door. Unable to see that the glass barrier is there, the bird has attempted to fly straight through and been killed by the force of the impact. Birds also sometimes attack their own reflection, believing that it is a rival male that has entered their territory. To try to prevent such collisions, fix a

silhouette of a hawk on the inner surface of a window or door, which hopefully will deter the bird from flying straight into the glass.

**Water:** water may be critical for a bird's survival, but it can also bring about an early death by drowning, so if you have a water butt in your garden to collect rainwater make sure it has a wooden plank across it where birds can perch if they are tempted to drink. Ponds and even bird baths can also present a hazard if they are badly constructed, so that the sides are steep and allow small birds to fall into deep water. For this reason you should always make sure that any bird bath or pond has gently sloping slides where smaller birds can stand as they drink or bathe, without the danger of falling straight in.

# TOWNS AND PARKS AND THEIR BIRDS

If you are already enjoying watching the birds that come into your garden, then you may now want to explore father afield, and get to know the birds in your local park or elsewhere in your village, town or city. You will immediately notice that although many of the birds you see are familiar species that also visit your garden, there are also others that you cannot immediately recognise. So as well as your binoculars you may also want to take this book or a more comprehensive field guide.

The birds you see in towns are usually more streetwise than you might give them credit for. Crows, magpies and pigeons are notorious scavengers, always ready to capitalise on food accidentally dropped by busy commuters or discarded scraps. Certain species of gull such as the Herring and Lesser Black-backed have started in recent years to build their nests on warehouse roofs.

Of course within towns, birds are most likely to head for open areas, so you could do a lot worse than start off in your local park: though an early start is a good idea as parks soon

become filled with dog-walkers, joggers and people on their way to work, which means the wildlife sometimes needs to keep a low profile. One of the advantages of a busy park, however, is that the wildlife soon gets used to the presence of human beings, and is usually much less shy than elsewhere. Birds like the Jay or Green Woodpecker may allow a surprisingly close approach as a result.

Winter is a good time to visit as there may be flocks of tits and sparrows, woodpeckers are often more visible (when there are no leaves on the trees), and even the smallest park lake or pond usually plays host to a variety of ducks. Beware, however, of park authorities' habit of releasing exotic wildfowl species, and don't get too excited if you see a duck you can't recognise – it has almost certainly been put there! Nevertheless, you may well see Tufted Duck, Pochard and Shoveler, all of which may have flown here from Siberia to spend the winter. They soon become used to human presence and will even take bread. Other water birds may include the Great Crested and Little Grebes (the latter also known as Dabchick on account of its diminutive size), Coot and Moorhen.

Parks often have slightly wilder areas, perhaps a meadow with longer grass, or a wooded patch. These 'mini-habitats' are also excellent for birds: in autumn and winter there may be Nuthatch or Treecreeper, like the woodpeckers easier to see than at other times of year; while in spring and summer these areas play host to a wide range of resident and breeding species and summer visitors. The former category includes familiar garden birds such as the Wren, Robin and Dunnock, and other species that prefer large areas of parkland such as Mistle Thrush. Some birds are harder to see, and you may need to get to grips with birdsong to identify them with certainty. Species commonly found in parks include Willow Warbler, Chiffchaff, Blackcap and Whitethroat, all of which have distinctive songs.

If there is a small stream, river or canal in the vicinity, take a walk along the banks. Early morning visits will usually produce a heron or two, and perhaps even a glimpse of a Kingfisher. Other 'wildlife corridors' include roadsides, railway embankments and scrubby areas of wood, all of which will act as communication routes for all kinds of birds. One important thing to remember: always think about your personal safety, and if you plan to be in a park or other local area very early or late in the day it is best to go with someone else.

If you want to explore farther afield than the boundaries of your local park, then check out the A to Z or Ordnance Survey map for areas which look promising, such as woodlands or gravel pits; or even local nature reserves. Or you can join your county bird club – ask at your library for details – who will run guided walks to local areas and also produce an annual report of bird sightings – you'll be amazed at what can be seen! If you find somewhere you really enjoy visiting then why not adopt it as your 'local patch'. If you visit the same place on a regular basis throughout the year you will really get to know your local birds thoroughly, and develop your skills and experience as a birdwatcher.

Whatever level you decide to watch birds – be it in your garden, local park or further afield – the most important thing is that you enjoy yourself. Ultimately that is what any pastime is for: so don't worry if you can't identify every bird you see or hear; the pleasure of birding is more about the aesthetic experience, and simply being out in the open air.

| J | F | M | A | M | J |
|---|---|---|---|---|---|
| J | A | S | O | N | D |

## ID FACT FILE

**SIZE**
Length 46-51cm
(18-20in).
Smaller and
more slender
than Mallard.

**LOOKALIKES**
Easy to spot in
breeding plumage.
In non-breeding
plumage it may
resemble smaller
grebes such as
the Red-necked.

**VOICE**
Variety of growling,
nasal calls, often
given in courtship
display; otherwise
usually fairly
quiet, except
when alarmed.

**FEEDING**
Feeds mainly on
fish, especially
minnows and
roach. Also takes
small aquatic
insects and
occasional
amphibians.
Food obtained by
diving.

# Great Creasted Grebe
*Podiceps cristatus*

This beautiful species was once heavily
persecuted, its plumes and skins being
used to supply the fashion trade.
Thankfully, a campaign led by Victorian
women managed to ban the killing, and
led to the forming of the RSPB. Today
this magnificent bird, the largest
European grebe, is protected and able to
live in peace, and pairs are a common
sight on ponds, rivers and lakes,
especially in southern Britain.

## Appearance
A slender, elegant waterbird, with a long,
narrow neck and flattened body, which
gives it a low-lying appearance in the
water. Adults have brown upperparts and
pale underparts; and during the breeding
season they sport a prominent crest in
various shades of brown and orange-
yellow, which they use for displaying to
each other. In winter they lose the crest
and appear much paler. Young birds are
striped black and white like a giant
humbug!

## Behaviour
Usually seen swimming elegantly on the
surface of the water, or diving down
beneath it to obtain food. Often seen in
pairs, especially during the breeding
season, with pair bonding and courtship
beginning as early as January. This
species' breeding display is complex and

Adult
(winter)

spectacular, with elaborate courtship rituals involving head shaking, and offering each other water weed in a ritualised dance.

## Breeding
Like all grebes, it builds a floating nest out of aquatic vegetation, usually anchored to the bank or a waterside bush or tree. The parents often cover the eggs with water weed to hide them from predators, which stains them green from their original white. Once hatched, the chicks often hitch a ride on their parents' back, where they can be surprisingly hard to see. Lays 2-6 eggs, incubated for 28 days. Young fledge after 10-11 weeks. Usually two broods.

## When & where
Common on suitable waterways in most of England apart from the south west; also found in parts of Wales, southern Scotland and Ireland. Resident.

GREBES

### ID FACT FILE

**Size**
Length 25-29 cm
(10-11.5 in)

**Lookalikes**
Most likely to be
mistaken for a
young duckling,
though darker
brown in colour
and with different
shaped bill.

**Voice**
Rapid, staccato
trill or repeated
notes; sounds
like high-pitched
laughter.

**Feeding**
Feeds on aquatic
invertebrates
such as
molluscs, and
small fish,
obtained by
diving.

# Little Grebe
*Tachybaptus ruficollis*

Our smallest species of grebe, which
although fairly common and widespread
in suitable habitats, often skulks on the
edge of ponds and lakes, sometimes
making it difficult to see. It is often heard
rather than seen: a loud and distinctive
trilling call gives its presence away. It is
also known as the 'Dabchick' because of
its resemblance to a young duck, for
which it is often mistaken.

## Appearance
Tiny: its size and shape mean that it is
easy to overlook or mistake for the young
of another waterbird. Very 'fluffy' in
appearance, as it tends to puff up its
feathers. Like all grebes, it has a
distinctively shaped bill: in this case short
and stubby. Plumage appears brownish-
grey, but is fairly dull outside the
breeding season. In breeding plumage,
however, it sports a dazzling chestnut
brown head and neck, and dark cap.

## Behaviour
Usually seen swimming at the edge of a
stream, pond or lake, often near the
safety of reeds or other vegetation, into
which it will retreat when threatened.
Dives beneath the surface to obtain its
food, bobbing up and down like a cork.
Rarely flies, but when it does so it
appears stumpy with short wings and a
round, pot-bellied body.

## Breeding

Like other members of the grebe family, it builds a
floating nest from water weed near the edge of the
water, usually hidden by vegetation, and attached to
branches or reeds to stop it floating away. The
young either ride on their parents' back for safety,
or return to the nest when danger appears.
Lays 3-6 white eggs (later stained
brown), incubated for 20 days.
Young fledge after 6-7 weeks.
Two to three broods.

## When & where

Found on streams, rivers, ponds and
lakes throughout lowland Britain,
though seen less frequently in towns
and cities than Great Crested Grebe,
preferring more suburban and rural areas.
Easily overlooked. Resident.

Adult
(winter)

| J | F | M | A | M | J |
| J | A | S | O | N | D |

### ID FACT FILE

**SIZE**
Length 80-100cm
(31-39in). Goose-
sized, but much
more slender.

**LOOKALIKES**
Given good views,
unmistakable;
though at coasts
may be confused
with the smaller
Shag, a pelagic
species rarely
found inland.

**VOICE**
A range of harsh,
throaty calls
uttered at the
nest site;
otherwise they
are mainly silent.

**FEEDING**
Feeds mainly on
large or small
fish, obtained by
deep diving,
which it swallows
whole.

# Cormorant

*Phalacrocorax carbo*

Once thought of mainly as a coastal species, in recent years the Cormorant has increased in numbers and has spread well inland, even starting to breed at some sites. It is most frequently seen outside the breeding season, when it may form quite large flocks on rivers and lakes. This has brought it into conflict with anglers, who claim that the Cormorant takes too many fish and should be controlled by shooting.

## Appearance

A large, mainly blackish-brown bird with broad wings and a long neck, giving it a distinctive silhouette when seen in flight or perched. Given closer views, the yellowish face patch and variable amounts of white on the belly become apparent. It often sits with wings outstretched in order to dry them, as unlike many other waterbirds, it lacks the ability to waterproof its feathers.

## Behaviour

A sociable species, often seen in flocks of anything from two or three to a couple of dozen birds, especially when drying its wings after feeding. Usually seen swimming on the water, where it dives deeply and for long periods to find food; also often seen in flight, where its black silhouette can give it a rather prehistoric, even sinister appearance.

CORMORANTS

Juvenile

## Breeding
Cormorants are social breeders, usually nesting in large colonies in the tops of trees, where they are safe from predators and can sound the alarm against any intruders. They build a large, untidy nest from twigs and lay 3-4 eggs, incubated for 30 days. Young fledge after about seven weeks. One brood.

## When & where
Once confined to coastal areas, but now found on rivers, lakes and large ponds throughout lowland Britain, though tends to be commoner in areas fairly near the coast or a large river. Also is often seen on rivers and reservoirs in cities such as London. Resident, though some local movements after breeding.

# Grey Heron
*Ardea cinerea*

### ID FACT FILE

**SIZE**
90-98cm (35-38in).
Very tall and
broad-winged.

**LOOKALIKES**
None likely to
cause confusion,
apart from the
Common Crane,
which is not
usually found in
towns and
gardens.

**VOICE**
A loud, deep and
gruff croak, often
uttered in flight –
sometimes
transcribed as
"fraaaank"!

**FEEDING**
Mainly eats fish
(almost any size
it can catch,
including goldfish
from a garden
pond) and other
aquatic life such
as frogs and
newts, which it
snatches using
that powerful bill.

The largest bird ever likely to visit your garden, the Grey Heron is most often seen at dawn and dusk, as it is a shy species and very wary of being disturbed. However, it can be tempted to make a lightning raid to snatch fish from a garden pond. The heron is also often seen in flight overhead, where despite its distinctive silhouette it is often mistaken for a large bird of prey.

### Appearance
A tall, statuesque bird, with a distinctive upright stance, and stately manner, especially when standing motionless to feed. It is mainly grey in colour, though paler beneath. A closer view reveals black on the head and wings, white on the face and neck, and a sharp, yellowish, dagger-shaped bill. Juvenile birds lack the black head markings. In flight it looks huge, with a hunched neck, broad wings and long, trailing legs.

### Behaviour
In towns and gardens it mainly comes to ponds, but elsewhere frequents rivers, streams and lakes. While hunting, it usually stands motionless, waiting patiently for some time before striking at its aquatic prey. The Heron is a shy bird, and will usually fly when disturbed, though with patience you can get good views.

HERONS AND STORKS

### Breeding

A colonial nester, breeding in
noisy 'heronries', usually at
the tops of large trees.
Builds a large, untidy nest from
sticks and breeds very early,
laying eggs in February or
March. Lays 3-5 greenish-blue
eggs, incubated for 25 days.
Young fledge after 7-8 weeks.
Usually one brood.

Adult

### When & where

Common and widespread in suitable wetland
habitats throughout lowland Britain and Ireland.
Currently increasing, and perhaps less shy than
formerly due to increased contact with human
beings. Resident.

| J | F | M | A | M | J |
| J | A | S | O | N | D |

## ID FACT FILE

**Size**
100-115cm
(39-45in). Huge!

**Lookalikes**
None apart from
the odd escaped
exotic species.

**Voice**
Usually silent,
apart from a very
loud bill
clattering when
the male and
female meet at
the nest, which
reinforces the
pair bond
between them.

**Feeding**
Feeds on a wide
variety of
amphibians,
beetles and
rodents, which it
seizes with that
large, powerful
bill. Regurgitates
food for the
young – not a
pretty sight!

# White Stork
*Ciconia ciconia*

A huge, handsome and stately bird,
known to generations throughout Europe
as the bringer of good luck and –
according to folklore – babies! Following
a rapid decline across its western
European breeding range the species is
now making a comeback, thanks largely
to homeowners who have built special
stork platforms for the birds to nest.

## Appearance
A very tall, upright, statuesque bird. Its
plumage is mainly a dirty, yellowish-
white (looking bright white at a distance),
with black wing tips and a large red bill.
In flight the broad white wings with their
darker wing tips and elongated neck are
very distinctive.

## Behaviour
Storks are sociable birds, often seen in
small family groups or flocks, especially
when feeding in fields. On migration,
they may form huge flocks comprising
several thousand birds, which head for
narrow bottlenecks of land between
continents such as the Straits of Gibraltar
or the Bosphorus, where they are able to
cross the sea safely.

## Breeding
The White Stork builds a huge nest out
of sticks on the roofs of houses, which
according to European folklore brings

HERONS AND STORKS

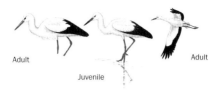

Adult

Juvenile

Adult

plenty of good luck to the householder. It will readily take to breeding on artificial platforms and lays 3-5 eggs, incubated for 5-6 weeks. Young fledge after 8-9 weeks. One brood.

## When & where

A summer visitor, flying from its African winter quarters to parts of southern and eastern Europe: still commonest in rural parts of Spain, Germany and various eastern European countries where traditional farming methods are still being practised. A very rare visitor to Britain, usually in spring, though storks often escape from zoos and private collections.

SWANS, GEESE AND DUCKS

| J | F | M | A | M | J |
|---|---|---|---|---|---|
| J | A | S | O | N | D |

## ID FACT FILE

**Size**
125-155cm
(49-61in). Our
largest and most
majestic bird.

**Lookalikes**
Whooper and
Bewick's Swans.
However, these
are unlikely to be
seen in towns, and
have yellow bills.

**Voice**
As its name
suggests,
generally silent –
apart from
hissing noisily
when approached
too closely.

**Feeding**
Feeds on small
aquatic vegetation
obtained by dipping
neck beneath
water. Also grazes
in wet fields. Also
takes bread – but
don't get too close
to that snapping
bill!

# Mute Swan
*Cygnus olor*

Europe's largest flying bird, the Mute
Swan is arguably our most stately and
majestic species, long celebrated for its
royal connections. Indeed every year we
still practise the ancient ritual of 'swan
upping' on the River Thames, where
birds are caught and marked with the
name of their 'owner'. Swans are haughty
creatures, with little fear of humans, and
can sometimes be aggressive – though
the oft-told story that they can break a
man's arm with one blow of their wing is
a myth!

### Appearance
Unmistakable! A huge, pure-white bird
with a deep-orange bill, which has a
protruding black 'knob' – much larger in
the male bird or 'cob' (the female is
known as a 'pen'). Cygnets are a dirty-
grey colour (the original 'ugly duckling')
gradually moulting to show variable
amounts of white once they are a few
months old.

### Behaviour
It is generally seen floating serenely
along a river or lake, though its legs may
be frantically paddling beneath the
surface of the water! In flight it makes a
whirring noise with its wings – but does
not call (hence the name 'mute' swan).
May sometimes be seen away from water
grazing in fields.

SWANS, GEESE AND DUCKS

## Breeding
Pairs for life, and builds a huge nest out of sticks, floating by the edge of a lake or river. Lays 5-8 huge eggs, incubated for five weeks. Young do not fly until they are 4-5 months old. One brood.

## When & where
Common throughout lowland Britain and Ireland. Generally found on large areas of open water, especially park lakes and rivers, from which it is able to take to the wing. Resident.

Adult

| J | F | M | A | M | J |
|---|---|---|---|---|---|
| J | A | S | O | N | D |

## ID FACT FILE

**SIZE**
90-100cm
(35-39in). Our
largest species
of goose, though
still dwarfed by
the Mute Swan.

**LOOKALIKES**
Can be confused
with 'grey geese'
when seen in
flight, but given
good views the
black neck is
distinctive.

**VOICE**
Loud, deep,
honking call,
often uttered in
flight.

**FEEDING**
Feeds mainly by
grazing on grass
and other
vegetation, using
its specially
shaped bill to
obtain the
choicest
morsels.

# Canada Goose
*Branta canadensis*

Originally from North America, the
Canada Goose was introduced to Britain
by rich landowners during the 17th and
18th centuries as a species of ornamental
waterfowl to decorate the gardens of our
stately homes. Since then it has adapted
well to modern life, and is now a familiar
sight in many towns and cities, where it
sometimes reaches pest proportions.
Hence it is less popular on this side of
the Atlantic than in the USA and Canada!

## Appearance
A large, bulky goose with mainly brown
plumage and paler shading on its
underparts and belly. Its best
identification feature is the distinctive
black neck and head, and the white face
patch. Goslings are yellowish in
appearance until their first moult.

## Behaviour
A noisy, sociable bird, almost always seen
in large flocks (apart from in the
breeding season, when it forms a pair to
defend a territory against all-comers). It
spends most of its time feeding – usually
by grazing on short grassy turf in parks
and by lakes or rivers – and can be
aggressive towards other waterfowl, even
driving them away.

## Breeding
Builds a large, bulky nest from twigs and

SWANS, GEESE AND DUCKS

Adult

other vegetation by the side of the water. Lays 5-6 eggs, incubated for 28-30 days. Young stay with parents and can fly after 6-7 weeks. One brood.

### When & where
From their original introduction sites in southern and central Britain, Canada Geese have spread out, and the species is now common and widespread in any suitable habitat throughout England and Wales. However, it remains fairly scarce in Scotland, and is found in just one or two places in Ireland. Resident.

| J | F | M | A | M | J |
|---|---|---|---|---|---|
| J | A | S | O | N | D |

## ID FACT FILE

**Size**
63-73cm
(25-29in). Size
of a Shelduck;
larger than a
Mallard.

**Lookalikes**
Given good views,
more or less
unmistakable.

**Voice**
Weird range of
quacks, hisses
and trumpeting
calls. Like other
waterfowl,
generally silent
while feeding.

**Feeding**
Feeds mainly on
vegetation,
including seeds,
grasses and
aquatic plants.

# Egyptian Goose
*Alopochen aegyptiacus*

Despite its name, this peculiar looking
bird is not in fact a goose at all, but
closely related to the Shelducks rather
than to the true geese. Originally from
Africa as its name suggests, a flock of
birds was allowed to fly free at a stately
home in north Norfolk, from which the
species has since spread to many sites in
southern and eastern England.

## Appearance
The Egyptian Goose is unlike any other
species of waterfowl. It has a unique
combination of brownish-yellow
plumage, with patches of white, green
and deep chestnut on the wings, and a
peculiar black mask across the face,
giving it quite an aggressive appearance.
In flight the most distinctive feature is
the bright-white wing patches.

## Behaviour
Like many other species of ducks and
geese, Egyptian Geese spend most of
their time feeding or sleeping. They can
also be quite aggressive to members of
their own and other wildfowl species,
especially during the breeding season.

## Breeding
It begins to breed much earlier than
many other waterfowl – sometimes having
young by February or March – and
usually nests beneath a bush, or even in a

SWANS, GEESE AND DUCKS

Adult

hole in the bank of a lake or
in a tree. It lays 8-9 eggs,
incubated for about four
weeks. The young remain
with the parents for a long time, and usually are not
able to fly until they are at least 10 weeks old. One
brood.

**When & where**
Until very recently this species could only be found
in a 'wild' state in parts of North Norfolk, close to
where they were originally introduced. However, in
the past decade or so the species has undergone a
major population explosion, and extended its range
into many other parts of eastern and south-eastern
England and the Midlands, including the London
parks. Resident.

| J | F | M | A | M | J |
|---|---|---|---|---|---|
| J | A | S | O | N | D |

## ID FACT FILE

**SIZE**
50-65cm
(20-26in). Our
largest and
bulkiest duck.

**LOOKALIKES**
Males can only
be confused with
the male
Shoveler;
females like
several other
female ducks,
especially the
Gadwall.

**VOICE**
Only the female
utters the
familiar quacking
sound – the
male's call is a
quieter grunt or
wheezing sound.

**FEEDING**
Omnivorous,
taking all kinds
of plant and
animal food –
and of course
'bread for the
ducks'!

# Mallard
*Anas platyrhynchos*

This species is the classic 'duck' – familiar
to us from our earliest years, as every
child is taken to feed the ducks at some
point in his or her early life! Often
overlooked because it is so common and
familiar, the male Mallard is a
particularly handsome bird; though it can
also show aggression, especially during
the breeding season, when attacks by
gangs of marauding males on lone
females are common.

## Appearance
The male is unmistakable, with his
bottle-green head, white collar, magenta
and grey plumage and a purplish-blue
'speculum' on his folded wing. The
female shows various subtle shades of
brown and black, though at a distance
appears plain brown; she also has a
purplish-blue speculum. In flight, the
Mallard appears bulky.

## Behaviour
Mallards are generally seen in pairs or
small flocks, and like other ducks seem to
spend most of their time feeding. They
do so by 'dabbling' or 'upending' – either
placing their bill just beneath the surface
of the water, or dipping their head right
under with their tail in the air. In
summer they generally sit around and
moult.

SWANS, GEESE AND DUCKS

Adult male

## Breeding

Breeds early; sometimes as
early as February if it has been
a very mild winter. Builds a
shallow nest from twigs and
grasses, lined with down for
warmth. Lays as many as a dozen
eggs, incubated for 27 days. Young swim
immediately, tagging along with their parents, but
do not fledge until they are about seven weeks old.
Usually one brood.

Adult
female

## When & where

Mallards are common and widespread throughout
Britain and Ireland – even on offshore islands and at
the coast. The species is very common in town and
city parks, and along large rivers. Resident.

| J | F | M | A | M | J |
| J | A | S | O | N | D |

# Shoveler
*Anas clypeata*

This species is named for its unique and extraordinary spoon shaped (or 'spatulate') bill, which it uses to sieve tiny morsels of food from just below the surface of the water in a distinctive feeding action. Although less common and widespread than the closely-related Mallard, it nevertheless often appears on lakes in town parks, especially in winter.

## ID FACT FILE

**SIZE**
Length 44-52cm (17-20.5in). Slightly smaller than Mallard.

**LOOKALIKES**
Male may be mistaken for Mallard; female more similar to female Mallard or Gadwall.

**VOICE**
Not the most vocal of ducks; a few quiet quacking sounds.

**FEEDING**
Although Shovelers occasionally 'up-end' in the manner of other diving ducks, generally filter feeds on tiny aquatic animals and plant material.

## Appearance
Given good views of the bill, both the male and the female are hard to confuse with any other species of duck. The male superficially resembles the male Mallard, but apart from its green head, the rest of the plumage is quite different: white chest and chestnut flanks are the most obvious features. The female is very similar in plumage to the female Mallard. In flight, the male's white belly, heavy bill and pale underwings are all distinctive field marks.

## Behaviour
A sociable and gregarious duck, often seen feeding in a tightly bunched flock, with each bird frantically filtering food through its bill. By congregating, these birds seem to maximise the amount of food available, probably by disturbing the water below. Unlike some other dabbling ducks, the Shoveler almost always feeds in the water rather than by grazing on land.

SWANS, GEESE AND DUCKS

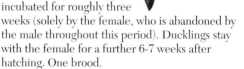

Adult male

Adult female

## Breeding

A scarce breeder in Britain. It builds its nest on the ground (but near water) and lays 8-12 eggs, incubated for roughly three weeks (solely by the female, who is abandoned by the male throughout this period). Ducklings stay with the female for a further 6-7 weeks after hatching. One brood.

## When & where

Has a more southerly distribution than most ducks and is fairly common throughout lowland parts of England and Wales: but is also found in parts of southern and eastern Scotland. Numbers augmented in winter by birds from the north and east. May be seen in towns, though shyer than the Mallard.

SWANS, GEESE AND DUCKS

| J | F | M | A | M | J |
|---|---|---|---|---|---|
| J | A | S | O | N | D |

# Wigeon
*Anas penelope*

## ID FACT FILE

**SIZE**
Length 45-51cm
(18-20in).
Smaller and
more compact
than Mallard.

**LOOKALIKES**
Male pretty
unmistakable;
female
superficially like
female Gadwall.

**VOICE**
Male gives
distinctive and
evocative
whistling call,
often in flight.
Female gives a
harsh growling
sound.

**FEEDING**
Feeds almost
entirely on plant
material,
obtained by
ducking its head
below water or
grazing.

This attractive and delightful dabbling
duck is a relatively uncommon breeding
bird in Britain, but a very common and
widespread autumn and winter visitor.
Birds from as far away as Scandinavia and
northern Russia spend the winter months
here, where thanks to our very mild
winter climate they can get plenty of food,
and are also relatively safe from predators.

## Appearance
A medium-sized, compact duck with a
distinctive shape. The male is very
obvious with his orange-brown head
contrasting with a bright, yellowish
forehead. He also has a pinkish breast, a
mainly grey body and a black tail,
creating a very pleasing combination of
shades and colours. The female is less
distinctive – though close views reveal a
subtle mixture of chestnut, grey and
brown – and is best identified by her bill
shape. In flight the white on the
upperwings of the male, and the white
belly of both sexes, are very obvious.

## Behaviour

Unlike most species of duck, the Wigeon
is often found grazing on short grass in
fields and meadows; plucking the
succulent tips of the grass as it goes. They
are very sociable birds, usually forming
large flocks and calling constantly to each
other even while feeding.

SWANS, GEESE AND DUCKS

### Breeding

A scarce breeding bird in Britain, confined mainly to Scotland and northern England. Lays 6-12 eggs, incubated for about 24 days (incubation is done solely by the female). Young become independent from their mother after about six weeks. One brood.

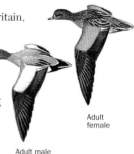

Adult female

Adult male

### When & where

Mainly a winter visitor to Britain from its breeding grounds to the north and east. In autumn and winter (from about September to March) it can be found on all suitable areas of water, especially those with shallow areas and grazing marsh nearby. Commoner near the coasts, especially on large marshes.

| J | F | M | A | M | J |
|---|---|---|---|---|---|
| J | A | S | O | N | D |

## ID FACT FILE

**SIZE**
Length 46-56cm (18-22in). A shade smaller than Mallard.

**LOOKALIKES**
Can be confused with several other ducks including Mallard, Wigeon and Teal.

**VOICE**
Male has deep croak; female a more chattering quack.

**FEEDING**
Feeds mainly on tiny morsels of plant matter, obtained by dabbling and up-ending on the surface of the water.

# Gadwall
*Anas strepera*

One of our least-known ducks, perhaps because at a distance males appear grey and females brown. Take a closer look, however, and you will see that the species is really attractive, with subtle shades of plumage and really fascinating behaviour.

## Appearance

A medium-sized dabbling duck, it is slightly smaller than a Mallard, with which it may be confused. Male appears grey but in fact has very subtly marked plumage – a mixture of black, grey and brown, with tiny 'vermiculations' giving a unique effect – and has a dark bill and distinctive black patch under the tail. The female is very like a female Mallard, but noticeably smaller and more compact, with an orange and brown bill. In flight the Gadwall is fairly nondescript and can be difficult to identify: look for pale underwings and the male's dark undertail.

## Behaviour

Usually 'dabbles' for food just beneath the water surface filtering morsels of food through its bill. Sometimes hangs around with Coots and diving ducks and picks disturbed morsels of food off the surface as they dive – whether or not the Coots gain any advantage from this association is not clear!

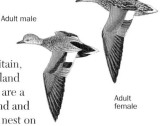

Adult male

Adult female

## Breeding

A scarce breeder in Britain, mainly confined to lowland England, though there are a few in southern Scotland and south Wales. Builds its nest on the ground, and lays 8-12 eggs, incubated for around 24 days (as in most dabbling ducks, by the female only). Young stay with their mother for about seven weeks after hatching. One brood.

## When & where

In autumn and winter the small breeding population is augmented by many thousands of birds which come here from the north and east, in search of a milder climate where they can be sure of finding enough food to survive. It may be seen on gravel pits and lakes on the edge of towns and cities, though is not usually found in the centre of urban areas.

SWANS, GEESE AND DUCKS

| J | F | M | A | M | J |
| J | A | S | O | N | D |

## ID FACT FILE

**SIZE**
Length 34-38cm
(13-15 in). Our
smallest duck;
half the weight
and bulk of
Mallard.

**LOOKALIKES**
Male very
distinctive;
female may be
mistaken for
other female
dabbling ducks,
but much
smaller.

**VOICE**
Male has a high-
pitched whistling
sound on two
notes; female
quacks rapidly.

**FEEDING**
Feeds on a wide
variety of animal
and plant items,
taken from
surface of water
or land.

# Teal
*Anas crecca*

Our smallest duck, the Teal is usually not
seen until it is flushed from its hiding
place in a small patch of water, marsh or
flooded field. One of our most delicate
ducks in both appearance and behaviour,
it is a favourite amongst birdwatchers.
The colour 'teal' (a bluish-green shade)
can be seen in the bird's eye patch.

## Appearance
Male stunningly beautiful, with his
combination of a chestnut head, green
patch over the eye, pale grey body, pale
stripe along the top of the flanks, and
yellow patch under the tail. Female less
colourful: basically brown with darker
markings which enable her to stay
camouflaged on the nest. Both sexes have
a small green patch (the 'speculum') on
the edge of the wing. In flight the Teal
appears tiny and with very fast wingbeats.

## Behaviour
Usually hangs around near the edge of
shallow water, often in pairs or small
groups; or hides in vegetation (such as a
reedbed). It also comes out to feed on
land, especially when a large area of mud
has been partially flooded. When startled
it will fly up very quickly, dashing away
on very fast beating wings before finding
refuge elsewhere. Teals can form quite
large groups, though they do not form
tight flocks as much as some other ducks.

SWANS, GEESE AND DUCKS

## Breeding

Builds its nest on the ground in thick vegetation, where it feels safe from predators, almost always very near water. Lays 8-11 eggs, incubated by the female only for about three weeks. The young stay with female for just over four weeks. One brood.

## When & where

Breeds mainly in lowland areas of northern Britain, though a few also breed in the south. Much more widespread outside the breeding season, when birds come here from continental Europe to spend the autumn and winter.

Adult female

Adult male

SWANS, GEESE AND DUCKS

| J | F | M | A | M | J |
| J | A | S | O | N | D |

## ID FACT FILE

**SIZE**
Length 40-47cm
(16-18.5in).
Medium-sized
duck, slightly
smaller than
Pochard.

**LOOKALIKES**
Male very
distinctive; only
the rarer Scaup
looks similar.
Female like
female Pochard
but darker.

**VOICE**
Male sometimes
gives a low
whistling sound,
usually during
courtship; female
a harsh cry.

**FEEDING**
Feeds on a wide
variety of animal
and plant items
obtained by
diving, and also
by grazing
ashore.

# Tufted Duck
*Aythya fuligula*

The commonest and best-known diving
duck in Britain, the Tufted Duck is found
in all sorts of places including lakes,
gravel pits, reservoirs and ponds in parks.
Numbers of breeding birds are swamped
by immigrants from northern Europe
and Siberia during the autumn and
winter. Both the male and female sport
the small tuft of feathers protruding from
the back of the head, which gives the
species its common name.

## Appearance
The male is very distinctive indeed: the
only common British duck to be all black
apart from white patches on the sides of
the body. The female and juvenile are
mainly mid-brown in colour, but with
paler patches on the flanks which are
similar to, though less obvious than, the
male's. Females also sometimes have a
pale patch around their beaks.

## Behaviour
A diving duck, which uses its powerful
legs to dive deep beneath the surface of
the water in search of food. As a result it
is generally found in more open areas of
deeper water than dabbling ducks such
as Mallard or Teal, and is often seen in
company with its close relative the Pochard.

## Breeding
Builds its nest out of grasses and reeds,

lined with down – usually on the
ground or at the edge of the
water. Lays 8-11 eggs,
incubated for roughly
25 days by the female
on her own (like most
other ducks). Young stay
with their mother for about
5-6 weeks, and fly soon
afterwards.

Adult male

Adult
female

## When & where
Although a widespread and fairly common breeding
bird in Britain, numbers increase in winter due to a
major influx of birds from Iceland and northern
Europe, which come to spend the winter here. In
autumn and winter, commonly found on waterways
throughout lowland Britain and some parts of Ireland.

SWANS, GEESE AND DUCKS

| J | F | M | A | M | J |
| J | A | S | O | N | D |

## ID FACT FILE

**SIZE**
Length 42-49cm (16.5-19in). Medium-sized duck, slightly larger than Tufted.

**LOOKALIKES**
Male fairly distinctive; female like paler version of female Tufted.

**VOICE**
Calls mostly weak and hard to hear at any distance, and generally only uttered during courtship.

**FEEDING**
Feeds on wide range of aquatic plant and animal matter, obtained by diving.

# Pochard
*Aythya ferina*

Along with the commoner Tufted Duck, this species is a 'diving duck', adapted to specialise in finding food in deep water. Like so many familiar species of duck it is easy to forget that this is actually quite a scarce breeding bird – it is much more familiar as a common autumn and winter visitor to Britain, generally found in large flocks on reservoirs and other areas of open water.

## Appearance
A large, bulky and slightly ungainly looking duck, with a distinctively large, long bill and a sloping forehead, which can help you identify the species even at a distance or in silhouette. The male is quite handsome, with a deep-chestnut head, black belly and grey body. The female is not at all distinctive: a dull greyish brown in colour with no obvious field marks. In flight, the male's pale belly and dark head and breast are obvious.

## Behaviour
Not a very inspiring duck: usually gathers in flocks of between a few dozen and several hundred birds, and seems to spend most of the time asleep. It occasionally rouses itself to dive deep beneath the surface to find food.

## Breeding
A very scarce breeder in Britain; mainly

SWANS, GEESE AND DUCKS

Adult female

confined to eastern
England and lowland
parts of Scotland. The
female builds a shallow cup
shaped nest near the water,
and lays 8-10 eggs, which she
incubates for 3-4 weeks.

Adult
male

Young stay with the female for
a while, but often become fully independent some
time before they can actually fly. One brood.

## When & where

In breeding season the Pochard is very scarce and
hard to find, but during the autumn and winter,
large numbers of birds come here from northern
and eastern Europe and northern Russia. At this
time the species becomes common and widespread
in eastern, southern and central Britain, but is
generally scarcer or absent elsewhere. It may be
seen on town lakes.

# Mandarin Duck

*Aix galericulata*

## ID FACT FILE

**SIZE**
Length 41-49cm
(16-19in).
Medium-sized,
neat and
compact.

**LOOKALIKES**
Can only be
confused with
the introduced
Wood or Carolina
Duck from North
America, which
has failed to
establish itself
here – females
very similar,
males only
superficially so.

**VOICE**
Various whistling
calls, generally
used in
courtship.

**FEEDING**
Feeds on wide
range of plant
and animal food
obtained in
various ways.

As its name suggests, this magnificent-looking duck was originally confined as a wild bird to China and Japan. It is another non-native, ornamental species, introduced into Britain in the 19th and early 20th centuries to add a splash of colour to parks and gardens, mainly in the Home Counties. Since then it has prospered and even spread to be found across much of southern England. It is one of the few 'alien' species to be universally welcomed here.

### Appearance
Male sports a wonderful combination of distinctive and unique shape and bright colours: green back, red bill, orange face, magenta breast and yellow sides; with orange 'sails' on his back. The female is a similar shape but much less brightly coloured: mainly greyish brown with paler markings. In flight the shape is distinctive, along with the pointed tail.

### Behaviour
A fairly shy bird, though when used to humans will sometimes venture close for food. It often hides in vegetation near the water's edge, and will allow very close approach until flushed. Sometimes perches in trees.

### Breeding
Nests in holes in trees, from which young

SWANS, GEESE AND DUCKS

Adult female

Adult male

must leap to the ground! Lays 9-12 eggs, incubated by the female only for about four weeks. The young leave the nest almost immediately and are able to feed and look after themselves, though they stay around the mother for another six weeks or so. One brood.

## When & where
Mainly confined to south-east England, near where the original feral population was first released, though small, self-contained populations are also found in parts of northern England and Scotland. Resident, rarely moving far from its breeding areas even in winter.

| J | F | M | A | M | J |
| J | A | S | O | N | D |

## ID FACT FILE

**Size**
Length 35-43cm (14-17in). Small and compact duck, slightly larger than Teal.

**Lookalikes**
Male unlikely to be confused with any other bird; female may be mistaken for young duck of another species.

**Voice**
Mainly silent, but during display male utters peculiar rattling sounds.

**Feeding**
Feeds on insect larvae and aquatic plants found by diving.

# Ruddy Duck
*Oxyura jamaicensis*

Like the Mandarin, the Ruddy Duck is a non-native species – but much more controversial. 'Ruddies' were accidentally introduced in the mid 20th century when a few of this North American species escaped from Peter Scott's Wildfowl Trust HQ at Slimbridge. Since then opinion has been divided about this introduced species, because it is alleged that they threaten the survival of a rare southern European relative, the White-headed Duck, with which they interbreed.

## Appearance
Male in full breeding plumage is unmistakable, with bright, brownish-red plumage, white cheeks, black cap and blue bill! The female is duller and browner, with a dark cap. Young males, and males in winter, resemble females but have white cheeks. Both have a 'stiff' tail sticking up at an angle, which males put to good use in their amazing courtship display.

## Behaviour
A very active and engaging little duck, seen diving for food, or bobbing up and down; especially during the breeding season. The male traps air in his breast feathers, then beats it rapidly with his bill, creating a drumming sound and presumably exciting the female with his display.

SWANS, GEESE AND DUCKS

Adult female

Adult male
(summer)

## Breeding
Builds nest out of reeds and leaves, usually hidden in dense aquatic vegetation near the edge of the water. Lays 6-10 eggs, incubated for 3-4 weeks. Young can swim and dive immediately, but do not fly for another 7-8 weeks. The female sometimes has a second brood if the conditions are suitable.

## When & where
The Ruddy Duck's main stronghold used to be the English Midlands, but in recent years it has spread north, east and south, and can now be found in south-east England, the north-east, and a few places in Wales and Ireland. Resident, though undertakes local movements in winter.

| J | F | M | A | M | J |
| J | A | S | O | N | D |

## ID FACT FILE

**SIZE**
Length 28-38cm
(11-15in).
Medium-sized,
compact looking
bird of prey.

**LOOKALIKES**
Superfically
similar to
Kestrel; also
sometimes
mistaken for
pigeon in flight!

**VOICE**
A high-pitched,
repetitive 'kew-
kew-kew-kew-
kew'.

**FEEDING**
Feeds almost
exclusively on
small birds,
especially
finches, tits and
sparrows; which
it catches by
seizing with its
powerful claws.

# Sparrowhawk
*Accipiter nisus*

This specialised hunting machine has bounced back following a major population crash during the 1950s and 1960s, when it was poisoned by the effects of the agricultural chemical DDT. Today, it is our commonest garden bird predator; though because of its habits it is not often seen. Despite its name, the Sparrowhawk hunts a wide variety of small birds, which it usually takes by surprise as they feed.

### Appearance
A medium-sized, powerfully built raptor, with a long tail, rounded wings and hooked beak. The male is often considerably smaller than the female, with a bluish back and rust-coloured underparts. The female is browner, with heavy barring on her chest. In flight both male and female can appear almost pigeon-shaped, though with stiffer wingbeats and a more streamlined appearance.

### Behaviour
Usually hunts by ambushing its prey from a bird feeder or the ground, grabbing it in its sharp talons before plucking its feathers with that powerful beak. It also soars high above gardens and parks, often flapping its wings followed by a short glide. However, it can be shy so is not always easily seen. Best looked for on warm, sunny days in spring, when it soars high above its territory.

## Breeding

Builds a large nest from
twigs, usually in the
dense foliage of a
mature tree. Lays
5-6 blotchy bluish-
green and white
eggs, incubated for five weeks.
Young fledge after 3-4 weeks. One brood.

Adult male
(from below)

Juvenile
(from below)

## When & where

Nowadays, Sparrowhawks are a common if elusive
resident in many of our cities, towns, villages and
suburbs – especially well-wooded ones that provide
plenty of cover for nesting and hunting. They can be
seen throughout lowland Britain and Ireland; often
visiting in gardens where there is the opportunity of
easy picking from bird tables and feeders. Numbers
are currently increasing after the population crash in
the mid 20th century. Resident.

| J | F | M | A | M | J |
|---|---|---|---|---|---|
| J | A | S | O | N | D |

## ID FACT FILE

**Size**
Length 36-48cm
(14-19in).
Noticeably larger
and bulkier than
Kestrel.

**Lookalikes**
Superficially like
the Hobby or
Merlin, but much
larger and more
well built.

**Voice**
Rarely calls apart
from near nest,
where male and
female may call
in alarm or
greeting.

**Feeding**
Feeds mainly on
birds caught in
flight by
'stooping' down
on them from
above.

# Peregrine
*Falco peregrinus*

The largest member of the falcon family
to breed in Britain, the Peregrine is
named after its tendency to wander the
skies at will. Built for strength and speed,
its short but powerful wings and deep
chest enable it to hunt its prey by
stooping down onto it from a great
height. In doing so it may reach
extraordinary speeds: measured at up to
180 miles per hour!

## Appearance
In flight it appears large and thick-set,
with broadly-based, pointed wings and a
deep chest, giving an impression of sheer
unadulterated power. When perched it
sits upright and surveys what is going on
around it with piercing eyes. A close look
will reveal mainly dark, bluish-grey
upperparts and paler underparts with a
dark streak. The dark cap and dark marks
on the cheeks, giving a masked appearance,
are also noticeable at close quarters.

## Behaviour
Hunts its prey in the air, soaring or
gliding around in search of a likely target,
then changing into capture mode. At this
stage it may either swoop low over a flock
of birds and try to pick off a sick or
injured individual; or fly high into the
sky, then stoop down on an unsuspecting
bird, hitting it at great force with its
powerful talons.

## Breeding

Nests on cliff
ledges, buildings
and sometimes in
old nests in trees.
Lays 3-4 eggs,
incubated for 4-5 weeks.
Young stay with their
parents for several
weeks after leaving
the nest.

Adult

## When & where

In the breeding season, Peregrines are found mainly
in upland areas, but in recent years the population
has increased, and
pairs are now
heading into towns
and cities where they
may breed on
prominent and well-
known buildings. In
autumn and winter
most birds head
down to lowland
areas such as coastal
marshes; though
some also spend the
winter in cities.
Resident.

| J | F | M | A | M | J |
|---|---|---|---|---|---|
| J | A | S | O | N | D |

## ID FACT FILE

**Size**
Length 30-36cm
(12-14in). Same
size as Kestrel
but appears
slimmer.

**Lookalikes**
Superficially like
Kestrel but
darker and more
rakish in
appearance.

**Voice**
Rapid, repeated
'kew kew kew'
call, often
uttered in mid-
air.

**Feeding**
Feeds on a
variety of bird
and insect food,
including
dragonflies,
usually caught in
flight.

# Hobby
*Falco subbuteo*

Unlike other British falcons, the Hobby
is purely a summer visitor to Britain,
arriving in late April or May and
departing south in September for its
winter quarters in Africa south of the
Sahara. This slim, delicate and attractive
falcon closely resembles the Swift, which
it often hunts. Once very rare in Britain
and confined to a few specialised
habitats, Hobbies have increased in
numbers and extended their range and
are now a relatively common sight in
southern Britain during the summer
months.

## Appearance
Slimmer and much darker in appearance
than the commoner Kestrel, with
noticeably narrower, more pointed wings.
Also has a very different flight action: its
slender build giving it a more
manoeuvrable appearance in the air. A
good view reveals dark-bluish upperparts
and paler underparts streaked dark; and a
distinctive rusty-orange patch under the
tail, which is often visible in flight.
Juveniles appear browner than their
parents.

## Behaviour
Especially during the spring and autumn,
Hobbies often hunt in small groups,
chasing and catching dragonflies or
House Martins in mid-air, snatching

BIRDS OF PREY

Adult
male

them with their powerful claws.
The best time to look for Hobbies
is on a fine, warm evening when
insects and birds are gathering;
especially near open water. No
other British falcon hunts in groups
in this way.

Adult
female

### Breeding
Builds its nest in a tall tree and lays 2-4 eggs,
incubated for 28-32 days. The young fledge and
leave the nest after about four weeks, but continue
to be dependent on their parents for food for some
time afterwards.

### When & where
Summer visitor, arriving in April and leaving in
August-September. Found in suitable heathland or
wetland habitat across most of southern England,
especially counties in the south and east. Hotspots
include Stodmarsh in Kent, the New Forest and the
Somerset Levels.

BIRDS OF PREY

| J | F | M | A | M | J |
|---|---|---|---|---|---|
| J | A | S | O | N | D |

## ID FACT FILE

**SIZE**
Length 32-35cm
(13-14in).
Medium sized
falcon.

**LOOKALIKES**
May be mistaken
for Sparrowhawk
(but slimmer) or
Hobby (but
bulkier).

**VOICE**
A far-carrying,
high-pitched and
repetitive 'kee-
kee-kee', often
uttered in flight.

**FEEDING**
Preys mainly on
small rodents
such as voles,
though also
takes small birds
and insects.
Hovers to catch
much of its food.

# Kestrel
*Falco tinnunculus*

Britain's commonest bird of prey hunts
by hovering over roadsides, fields and
verges. Originally a bird of the open
countryside, in recent years the Kestrel
has adapted well to living alongside
human beings, often nesting on the
roofs of buildings. It is also a common
sight as it hunts over the edges of
motorways. It usually catches its prey by
hovering or by pouncing down from a
perch.

## Appearance
Best identified in flight, by its slim,
streamlined shape, with slender, pointed
wings and long tail. The male is smaller
than the female, with pale-grey head,
black moustaches and a russet-orange
back covered with small black spots. The
female is bulkier, with a darker, chestnut
back streaked (not spotted) with black.
In flight the male shows darker wing tips
contrasting with a lighter back.

## Behaviour
Kestrels have a characteristic habit of
hovering in one position, head
motionless, in search of their rodent
prey. This common behaviour once gave
it the folk name of 'windhover'. It flies
fast and direct, though occasionally soars
on broader wings, when it may be
mistaken for a Sparrowhawk given poor
views. In winter it tends to hunt by

BIRDS OF PREY

Adult male

perching, staying motionless (and often surprisingly hard to see) in one place before dropping down on its unsuspecting prey.

### Breeding

Nests in tree holes and on roofs in towns and cities. Lays 3-6 pale eggs, blotched with reddish-brown, which are incubated for four weeks. Young fledge after 4-5 weeks. One brood.

### When & where

Resident. Found throughout Britain and Ireland apart from the extreme north and west. Common in farmland habitats and along roadsides, especially motorway verges. Currently decreasing, especially in the open countryside, where there are fewer prey items thanks to modern farming methods.

GAME BIRDS

| J | F | M | A | M | J |
|---|---|---|---|---|---|
| J | A | S | O | N | D |

## ID FACT FILE

**SIZE**
Length 53-89cm
(21-35in). Male
much longer than
female due to
the length of his
tail-feathers.

**LOOKALIKES**
Female may be
mistaken for
Partridge given
poor views. Male
unmistakable.

**VOICE**
Loud, far-carrying
croaking call.

**FEEDING**
Feeds on wide
variety of grains,
seeds and
various items
picked up from
the ground.

# Pheasant
*Phasianus colchicus*

Originally introduced from south-west
Asia to Britain, almost certainly by the
Romans (who brought it as a food
supply), the Pheasant has thrived in the
woodland and farmland habitats of the
English countryside. Today it has the
dubious honour of being our most
hunted game bird, with millions being
shot each year – many of which are, in
fact, artificially bred and released purely
for this purpose.

## Appearance
The male Pheasant is quite simply
unmistakable, with a bottle-green head,
rich reddish-brown plumage, and a very
long tail. Some show a white ring around
the neck. The female is plumper, paler
and less colourful, with a much shorter
tail to aid camouflage (especially when
sitting on eggs or guarding her young).

## Behaviour
Pheasants are shy, wary birds –
understandably so given that they face
the prospect of being shot! They often
skulk around the edge of a field, or
sometimes venture into the open to feed,
especially outside the shooting season.
They also feed in the undergrowth in
woodland. When the young are born,
females are careful to avoid the open,
where the chicks may be vulnerable to
predators.

GAME BIRDS

Adult male         Adult female

## Breeding
Breeds in dense cover
on the edge of a field
or in a wood. Lays
8-15 eggs (reports of
up to 25 are usually the result of two females
laying in the same nest), incubated for 3-4 weeks.
Young are brooded by the female, and become
independent several months after hatching.

## When & Where
Common and widespread throughout lowland
Britain and Ireland, apart from the extreme north
and west, generally in traditional countryside with
a mixture of farms and woods. However, will also
turn up in the most unexpected places, including
on the edge of built-up areas. Resident, rarely
travelling very far from where they are born
and reared.

RAILS

| J | F | M | A | M | J |
| J | A | S | O | N | D |

# Coot
*Fulica atra*

## ID FACT FILE

**Size**
Length 36-38cm
(14-15in). Size of
medium-sized
duck.

**Lookalikes**
Moorhen, which
is browner in
colour and has
red and yellow on
bill.

**Voice**
A series of odd
but distinctive
single note calls.

**Feeding**
Feeds on all
kinds of aquatic
material, mainly
plants, obtained
by picking off the
surface, or by
diving.

Though it superficially resembles a duck,
the Coot is in fact a member of the rail
family, which has adapted to swimming
rather than walking. It is one of the most
familiar of British water birds, found in
all kinds of places including village ponds
and lakes in the centre of towns and
cities. Its partially webbed feet enable it
to dive deep beneath the surface of the
water in order to find food.

## Appearance
The only all black water bird, though if
you get very close it is possible to see that
the 'black' includes subtle shades of dark
grey. The Coot's most distinctive feature
is its white bill and facial patch. It can
easily be told apart from its close relative
the Moorhen by its larger size and lack of
red or yellow on bill. Chicks have red on
their heads, which can lead to confusion
with baby Moorhens.

## Behaviour
Usually seen on the water, around
shallow ponds, rivers or lakes. Like a
duck, it either dabbles or dives in search
of food. Often forms a loose association
with dabbling ducks such as the Gadwall,
which appears to take advantage of the
Coot's ability to disturb the water and
bring small food items to the surface.
Coots can be quarrelsome birds,
especially during the breeding season.

## Breeding

Builds a floating nest of vegetation, either by the bank of a lake or river, or on a small offshore island, often in full view. Lays 6-10 eggs, incubated for 21-24 days. Young stay with parents for another 4-5 weeks, before flying at approximately eight weeks. Two, sometimes three, broods.

## When & Where

Common throughout lowland Britain apart from extreme south-west and north and west Scotland. A familiar sight on any small body of water, including park lakes. Resident.

Adult

RAILS

| J | F | M | A | M | J |
| J | A | S | O | N | D |

## ID FACT FILE

**SIZE**
Length 32-35cm (12.5-14in).

**LOOKALIKES**
Superficially resembles Coot; told apart by smaller size, red and yellow bill and more colourful plumage.

**VOICE**
A range of clucking calls, including a repetitive 'ki-ki-ki-kik'.

**FEEDING**
Feeds on a wide variety of underwater invertebrates, picked from off or just beneath the water surface, or from wet grass.

# Moorhen
*Gallinula chloropus*

Although a member of the rail family, the Moorhen, along with its close relative the Coot, is more like a duck in appearance and habits. Although shy and unobtrusive, it is a widespread and familiar bird, often found on ponds in parks and villages. The name 'Moorhen' is in fact derived from the words 'mere hen' – simply meaning 'bird of the ponds'.

## Appearance

Superficially resembles a small duck, but can easily be distinguished by its habit of bobbing while swimming, and by its distinctive red and yellow bill, which is pointed rather than flattened like that of a duck. Adults are dark bluish-brown, with greyer flanks, and a pale line of feathers dividing the upperparts and underparts. Look out for a noticeable pale patch behind the cocked tail. The sexes appear similar, but the juvenile is much browner in appearance, and lacks the colourful bill, although still shows a white patch under its tail, which is diagnostic.

## Behaviour

Often seen swimming along with its distinctive jaunty gait, or hiding shyly on the edge of reeds or aquatic vegetation. It also feeds on areas of wet grass, including lawns near streams or ponds. Unlike Coot, it does not dive. It rarely takes to the wing, usually only for a short flight

RAILS

across the surface of the
water, with its legs trailing
behind.

Adult

### Breeding
Builds a floating nest at
the edge of a pond or lake,
where it lays an average of seven eggs
(often more), incubated for three
weeks. Young fledge after 6-7 weeks, but
can swim immediately after hatching,
though they continue to be fed by their parents for
up to six weeks. Two or three broods.

### When & where
Found on small areas of fresh water, including
ponds, rivers and lakes, throughout lowland Britain
and Ireland apart from the extreme north and west.
Population currently stable. Resident.

| J | F | M | A | M | J |
|---|---|---|---|---|---|
| J | A | S | O | N | D |

## ID FACT FILE

**SIZE**
Length: 35-39cm
(14-15in). One of
our smallest
gulls: slightly
larger than a
pigeon.

**LOOKALIKES**
Common Gull:
which is larger,
with an all-white
head and
greenish legs.

**VOICE**
Like all gulls,
noisy and
quarrelsome.
Gives a range of
loud, raucous
calls.

**FEEDING**
Wide range,
including worms,
bread and
household food
waste,
scavenged from
rubbish tips. An
opportunistic
feeder, snatching
scraps from
other birds.

# Black-Headed Gull
*Larus ridibundus*

This familiar species is our commonest
and most widespread gull, especially
inland. In recent years it has learned to
live alongside human beings, scavenging
for food on rubbish-tips, and in town and
city parks, where it is generally the
commonest member of its family. In
spring, most birds head away from urban
areas to breed, before returning in large
flocks for the autumn and winter.

## Appearance
In spring and summer, it can easily be
told apart from other gulls by its
chocolate-brown hood – all other
common species of gull have white
heads. Breeding plumage may be
attained as early as the New Year for
some individuals. Outside the breeding
season, it can be identified by its smaller
size, pigeon-shaped appearance and dark
spot behind the ear. In flight it has
pointed wings, edged with white and
tipped with black.

## Behaviour
A sociable bird, often gathering in large,
noisy flocks to feed or rest, in open grassy
areas such as parks and school playing-
fields. These gulls squabble with each
other over food, especially when raiding
feeding stations in gardens, where they
are regular visitors. They roost in huge
flocks with other gulls on urban

GULLS AND TERNS

reservoirs, and can often be seen
flying to and from feeding
areas at dawn and dusk, in a
loose V-formation.

Adult
(winter)

## Breeding
Breeds mainly in large, noisy
colonies, in general away from
towns and cities. Lays 2-3 bluish-green
eggs, blotched with brown and grey, which
it incubates for 22-24 days. Young fledge after
5-6 weeks. One brood.

## When & where
Found throughout Britain and Ireland, though
most likely to be seen in urban areas in autumn,
winter and early spring, when large flocks come
in to towns and cities to feed and roost. Resident.

GULLS AND TERNS

| J | F | M | A | M | J |
| J | A | S | O | N | D |

### ID FACT FILE

**SIZE**
Length 40-42cm (16-16.5in). A medium sized gull.

**LOOKALIKES**
Superficially similar to Herring Gull, but smaller and slightly darker grey; or to Black-headed, but larger and with white head.

**VOICE**
A mewing call that gives it the alternative name 'Mew Gull'.

**FEEDING**
Feeds mainly on invertebrates and small fish, obtained from the land or water.

# Common Gull
*Larus canus*

Despite its name, this is not our most common gull, either on the coasts or inland, though in autumn and winter it is fairly widespread. In fact many people believe that the name 'Common' Gull derives from its habit of feeding on common land, rather than being an indication of its status. It is much more widespread in winter, when the British population increases by more than six fold.

## Appearance
A handsome, medium-sized gull with an all-white head, belly and underparts, mid-grey back and wings and greenish bill and legs. Like most familiar gulls it also has black wingtips. It is often best told by its distinctive 'friendly' appearance, due to its rounded head. In winter it can show variable amounts of darkish speckling on the head. In flight it has more rounded wings than the Black-headed Gull, and appears smaller and more compact than the larger gulls. Immature birds show variable amounts of brown feathering on their back and wings.

## Behaviour
Often joins flocks of Black-headed Gulls to forage on playing fields or in gardens. Towards dusk it will fly off from its feeding areas to roost, forming characteristic 'flight lines' along with other gull species. It roosts mainly on

GULLS AND TERNS

reservoirs, sometimes in
mixed flocks of several
thousand birds.

Adult
summer

### Breeding
Breeds in colonies in remote parts
of northern Britain. Lays 2-5 eggs,
incubated by both parents for 3-4
weeks. Young leave the nest after a few
days but continue to hang around with
the adults for about five weeks. One brood.

### When & Where
During the breeding season it is mainly
confined to colonies in the north of Britain,
especially Scotland. In autumn and winter it can
be found throughout Britain, though tends to be
commoner near coasts. Usually associates with
other gull species, especially the smaller Black-
headed Gull.

Second
winter

| J | F | M | A | M | J |
| J | A | S | O | N | D |

# Herring Gull
*Larus argentatus*

## ID FACT FILE

**Size**
Length 55-67cm
(21.5-26in). One
of our largest
gulls.

**Lookalikes**
Common Gull,
though this
species is
smaller and with
a darker grey
back.

**Voice**
The classic
honking 'seagull'
call, either
uttered in flight
or from a perch.

**Feeding**
Feeds on almost
anything – fish,
roadkill,
unmentionable
stuff scavenged
from rubbish
dumps – a true
21st century bird.

This species is the classic 'seagull' with which generations of children have become familiar from summer holidays by the seaside. Herring Gulls are large, noisy and seem to be always looking for trouble! In recent years there has been a major population shift away from the coast and inland, perhaps because of declines in fish stocks. Nowadays the species has even begun to move into city centres to breed, nesting on the roofs of tall buildings.

## Appearance
A large gull, intermediate in size between Lesser and Great Black-backed Gulls. In the breeding season it has a bright white head, and white underparts, pale grey back and pinkish legs – a useful identification feature. The bill is yellow with a red spot (used to stimulate the chick to peck for regurgitated food). In winter it often shows variable amounts of dark speckling on the head, giving a rather messy appearance. The young appear various shades of brown.

## Behaviour
Gregarious and opportunistic, always on the lookout for an easy meal, it has been known to swoop down and snatch ice-creams or fish and chip suppers from unsuspecting tourists! A sociable bird, its closeness to others often leads to noisy squabbling over food and territory.

GULLS AND TERNS

**Breeding**
Generally breeds in large
colonies, though in recent years
also in smaller groups in unusual
places such as city centres. Usually
lays 2-4 eggs, and incubates for 28-30
days. Young leave the nest a couple of
days after hatching, but are dependent
on their parents for food for several weeks
afterwards.

Adult
(summer)

**When & where**
Breeds mainly on coasts, but more and more now
do so on city roofs, sometimes well inland. Much
more common and widespread in winter when it
joins other gulls in flocks to feed and roost, and is
seen in large numbers inland. Resident.

| J | F | M | A | M | J |
|---|---|---|---|---|---|
| J | A | S | O | N | D |

## ID FACT FILE

**SIZE**
Length 52-67cm (20.5-26in). A fairly large gull, though usually slightly smaller and more compact than Herring Gull.

**LOOKALIKES**
Similar to Great Black-backed Gull, but generally smaller and with a slightly greyer back and wings.

**VOICE**
Similar to Herring Gull, but slightly deeper in tone.

**FEEDING**
Feeds on most things, including fish and scraps taken from rubbish dumps.

# Lesser Black-Backed Gull

*Larus fuscus*

The Herring Gull's smaller, neater relative has also adapted well to living alongside human beings, and like that species has begun to nest on city centre roofs in some numbers. Once mainly a summer visitor to Britain, in recent years it has adapted to the availability of food throughout the year and has stayed here right through the winter. It is more inclined to venture inland than the other large gulls, and is often seen on playing fields or in town parks.

**Appearance**
A medium to large gull, with a bright white head and underparts contrasting with its dark back – sometimes almost black, but more often than not dark grey in colour. Its yellow legs are a good identification feature, compared to the pinkish legs of its two larger relatives and generally looks more attractive than other large gulls. Young birds show variable amounts of brown in their plumage, and may have pinkish legs.

**Behaviour**
A bit more fastidious than the Herring Gull, though still highly adaptable to living alongside humans. Like all gulls, it has adapted to life in the 21st century, and is able to find food from a wide range of sources. A noisy, sociable bird, well worth taking a closer look at.

GULLS AND TERNS

Adult
(summer)

Second
summer

Juvenile

## Breeding
Breeds mainly in
colonies on coasts,
but in recent years it has colonised
roofs in city centres. Usually lays
three eggs (though can be as few as
one or as many as four), incubated
for 24-27 days by both parents. The young
leave the nest when they are only a few days
old, but hang around with their parents,
being fed by them, for another few weeks.

## When & where
Breeds mainly in colonies around our coasts. In
winter it can be found over much of southern
Britain, especially near cities. Generally less
marine than Herring Gull.

| J | F | M | A | M | J |
|---|---|---|---|---|---|
| J | A | S | O | N | D |

## ID FACT FILE

**Size**
Length 31-35cm
(12-14in). Size of
a small gull, but
has much longer
and narrower
wings and tail.

**Lookalikes**
May be mistaken
for a gull, but far
more elegant
and buoyant.

**Voice**
Loud, high-
pitched screech,
often uttered in
flight.

**Feeding**
Feeds mainly on
small fish, caught
by plunging into
the water.

# Common Tern
*Sterna hirundo*

Once mainly a bird of the coasts and the seaside, in recent years this beautiful summer visitor to Britain has adapted to nesting inland, using specially built rafts on lakes, reservoirs and gravel pits. Its harsh, raucous call is now a familiar sound of spring and summer along many of our waterways, including rivers and canals. Often nests in colonies of several dozen birds – a noisy spectacle!

### Appearance
A slim, elegant bird, superficially resembling a small gull but much more graceful – once memorably described as 'a gull that's died and gone to heaven!' It has a black cap (not a brown hood like the Black-headed Gull), pale-grey wings and black-and-white underparts. In flight or perched, its long tail streamers are always obvious – earning the species the folk name of 'sea swallow'.

### Behaviour
Hunts by flying in a buoyant manner over water, on the lookout for food. When it spots something suitable it plunges down to pick a morsel off the surface of the water. The courtship display often involves several males chasing a female.

### Breeding
Breeds in colonies on the coast, and also on inland wetlands. Lays 1-3 eggs,

Adult
(summer)

incubated for about three weeks. Young leave the
nest after a few days and fly after about four weeks,
but stay with their parents until they are 2-3 months
old, when they finally become fully independent.

**When & Where**
Summer visitor, usually arriving back to Britain from
its African winter quarters in mid to late April, and
departing in August or September. It is found
mainly around the coasts, but also breeds inland in
parts of eastern and southern England. On
migration, it may be seen on any stretch of open
water, such as reservoirs and gravel pits.

PIGEONS AND DOVES

| J | F | M | A | M | J |
|---|---|---|---|---|---|
| J | A | S | O | N | D |

### ID FACT FILE

**SIZE**
Length 31-34cm
(12-13.5in).
Noticeably
smaller than
Wood Pigeon.

**LOOKALIKES**
Similar to Wood
Pigeon and Stock
Dove.

**VOICE**
A familiar, three
noted cooing
sound.

**FEEDING**
Can eat virtually
anything even
remotely edible –
and occasionally
pretty inedible!

# Feral Pigeon
*Columba livia*

A largely despised and neglected bird,
the Feral Pigeon originally descended
from the wild Rock Dove, and was
domesticated by our ancestors for food
and sport. Today it has become a
familiar, though not always welcome,
sight in our towns and cities, where it
lives happily alongside human beings. Its
ancestor the Rock Dove is unfortunately
declining, partly as a result of
interbreeding with its feral relatives. If
you want to see a wild Rock Dove, you
will have to head to the extreme north
and west of the British Isles (see map).

### Appearance
Feral Pigeons show a bewildering variety
of different plumage features, with basic
colours ranging from white, through
browns and blacks, to the most typical
grey of the wild ancestor. Many show two
dark wing-bars and a white rump – a
distinctive feature, especially when seen
in flight. Feral Pigeons can cause a
hygiene problem if large numbers visit
gardens to feed, so it is best not to
encourage them by putting out food on
the ground.

### Behaviour
A highly sociable bird, almost always seen
in flocks, sometimes numbering many
hundreds of birds. It shows fascinating
breeding behaviour, with males

PIGEONS AND DOVES

Adult

performing courtship display
to females, especially in early
spring and summer.

## Breeding
Nests in holes and crevices, mainly in old buildings
in urban and industrial areas. In some urban areas
it is confined to the original Victorian part of the
city. Lays two white eggs, incubated for 2-3 weeks.
Young fledge after 4-5 weeks. It is very productive,
breeding almost all year round, with up to six
broods. Fledged young resemble their parents –
hence the answer to the question, 'why do you
never see a baby pigeon?'

## When & where
Found throughout lowland Britain, especially in
towns and cities, though much more localised in
Scotland and Ireland. The population is currently
stable. Resident.

PIGEONS AND DOVES

## ID FACT FILE

**SIZE**
Length 32-34cm
(12.5-13.5in).
Smaller and
slimmer than
Wood Pigeon

**LOOKALIKES**
Resembles small
Wood Pigeon but
lacks white
marks on neck
and wings.

**VOICE**
A soft pair of
notes, repeated
several times.
Less raucous and
more pleasant
sounding than its
relatives.

**FEEDING**
Mainly eats
seeds, taken
from the ground.

# Stock Dove
*Columba oenas*

This shy, unobtrusive and often
overlooked member of the pigeon family
is found throughout much of Britain, and
may be seen in parks and gardens,
especially in rural and semi-rural areas.
Look out for pairs displaying in early
spring, or small groups of birds feeding in
fields in late summer, after they finish
breeding.

## Appearance
The Stock Dove always looks slightly
smaller and more delicate than its larger
and commoner relative, the Wood Pigeon.
It has a slightly darker, more steel-grey
plumage, with wings and tail tipped with
black – obvious to see when in flight. It
has a delicate yellow bill with a red base,
and a purplish green sheen on its neck,
which is also quite distinctive, especially
given good close views. In flight it
appears 'squarer-winged' than other
pigeons, and lacks any white on the wing.

## Behaviour
Can be shy and elusive, often sitting
quietly in the branches of a tree, so is
easy to miss. It will also feed in open
areas, sometimes in flocks with other
pigeon species, where identification is
made easier by a direct comparison. In
spring males and females pair up and
undertake a distinctive display flight from
the tops of large trees.

PIGEONS AND DOVES

Adult

**Breeding**
Stock Doves breed from
late winter to late
autumn, nesting in holes in
trees, and laying two white
eggs, incubated for 16-18 days.
The young fledge after 3-4
weeks. Stock Doves are prolific
breeders, which may have up to five
broods in a single breeding season.

**When & where**
Found in suitable wooded and farmland habitat
throughout lowland England, Wales and the south
of Scotland, and also in the south and east of
Ireland. Not usually seen in upland areas. Generally
increasing after a decline during the middle of the
last century. Resident.

| J | F | M | A | M | J |
|---|---|---|---|---|---|
| J | A | S | O | N | D |

## ID FACT FILE

**SIZE**
Length 40-42cm (16-16.5in). Our largest pigeon.

**LOOKALIKES**
Usually distinguishable from other pigeons and doves by its large size and distinctive markings.

**VOICE**
A distinctive, monotonous, five-note call: 'coo-COO-coo, coo-coo' – with the stress on the second syllable.

**FEEDING**
Natural food includes seeds, berries and shoots, but will also take a variety of foods provided by humans.

# Wood Pigeon
*Columba palumbus*

Although originally a bird of the open countryside, Wood Pigeons have rapidly adapted to life in towns and cities, and are now as familiar a sight in town parks and squares as their feral relative. They are also a very frequent and common visitor to gardens, where they feed readily beneath bird tables and feeders, picking up spilt seeds from the ground. They will also visit bird tables, where they can cause havoc amongst the smaller birds! With their distinctive five-note call, they are one of the most familiar sounds of our towns and suburbs.

## Appearance
Our largest and bulkiest pigeon, easily identified by a combination of field marks. Look out for the distinctive white patch on the neck, the greyish plumage and reddish-purple coloured breast. In flight, it can easily be told apart from all other British species of pigeon and dove by the white stripes on its wings, which are visible even at a great distance. Young wood pigeons lack the adults' white patch on neck, and can be mistaken for Stock Doves.

## Behaviour
Although Wood Pigeons readily visit gardens and are found in most towns and cities, they can be shy and nervous, flying away as soon as they are disturbed. This

PIGEONS AND DOVES

is mainly because it is
still legal to shoot
them on farmland, so
they need to be wary!

Adult

**Breeding**
Like other pigeons, it breeds
throughout the year, building a
messy nest from twigs in a tree or
bush. Lays two white eggs, incubated
for 16-17 days. Young fledge after 3-5 weeks.
Usually have two broods.

**When & where**
Found throughout Britain and Ireland apart from
the extreme highlands and islands. Wood Pigeons
are currently thriving, with numbers increasing
rapidly. As a very adaptable species they are likely
to benefit from global warming. Resident.

| J | F | M | A | M | J |
|---|---|---|---|---|---|
| J | A | S | O | N | D |

## ID FACT FILE

**SIZE**
Length 31-33cm
(12-13in). Much
smaller than
Wood Pigeon.

**LOOKALIKES**
Given good views
very hard to
confuse with any
other pigeon or
dove.

**VOICE**
A distinctive,
though rather
monotonous,
three-noted call,
'coo-COO-coo',
with the stress
on the middle
syllable. Also a
loud screech.

**FEEDING**
Like other
pigeons and
doves, has a
marked
preference for
seeds.

# Collared Dove
*Streptopelia decaocto*

Incredibly, this familiar and attractive
little dove was not even a member of the
British avifauna until the mid 1950s.
Then, the very first birds arrived and
began to breed on the east coast, after a
very rapid spread across Europe from
western Asia. Having colonised and
spread throughout Britain and Ireland,
the Collared Dove is now one of the most
familiar birds of our towns, villages and
suburban gardens.

## Appearance
It can easily be told apart from other
doves and pigeons by its pale, pinkish-
brown plumage and the distinctive dark
collar which gives the species its name. It
has dark wingtips, is dark under the tail,
and has white outer tail-feathers, which
are often noticeable in flight, and are a
good field mark – especially if the bird is
flying away from you! It can easily be
attracted to garden feeding stations by
providing good quality seeds such as
sunflower hearts, either placed on a bird
table or scattered on the ground.

## Behaviour
In suburban areas it often sits on roofs or
fences, or visits bird tables and garden
lawns in search of food. Collared Doves
spend much of their time in pairs or
small groups, cooing to each other!

PIGEONS AND DOVES

### Breeding

It can nest all year round, though usually from February to October. It builds its nest from sticks in thick foliage, and lays two white eggs, incubated for 14-18 days. Young fledge after 2-3 weeks. Like other pigeons, it can have several broods in a single breeding season – a factor that allowed the species to colonise Britain so rapidly.

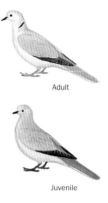

Adult

Juvenile

### When & where

Found throughout lowland England, Scotland and Wales, though far more thinly distributed in Ireland. Prefers to nest in leafy towns and suburbs, with plenty of trees and hedges, so may often be absent from busy city centres. Currently increasing. Resident.

| J | F | M | A | M | J |
| J | A | S | O | N | D |

## ID FACT FILE

**SIZE**
Length 38-42cm
(15-16.5in).
Slightly smaller
than a Magpie.

**LOOKALIKES**
Unlikely to be
confused with
anything other
than another
escaped species
of parakeet!

**VOICE**
A loud, high-
pitched screech,
usually uttered
as a contact call
in flight. Can
also utter a
repeated call
reminiscent of
that of the Green
Woodpecker.

**FEEDING**
Eats a variety of
fruits, berries
and seeds.

# Ring-Necked Parakeet
*Psittacula krameri*

This species was originally introduced
by accident in the early 1970s, when a
number escaped or were deliberately
released at various locations around
London. In the past 30 years or so, this
brightly-coloured Asian parakeet has
established a firm foothold in the
London suburbs, where it thrives in our
parks and gardens. The jury is out on
whether or not it will have a detrimental
effect on our native birds, by taking over
nest sites. Food-wise, it has a marked
preference for monkey nuts in their
shells, which it breaks open to get at the
peanuts inside. Indeed, without the help
of people who feed birds in their garden
it is possible that this exotic species
would never have found a toehold in
Britain.

## Appearance
Unmistakable: the only bright-green bird
in Britain, apart from the occasional
escaped parrot or parakeet from an
aviary! Long and very slender, with thin,
pointed wings and a hooked bill. Adults
have a dark ring around the collar, edged
with pink on males, which is visible given
a good close view.

## Behaviour
A noisy, sociable bird, often seen flying
overhead in large flocks. It roosts in
huge gatherings of up to several

thousand birds, usually in tall trees such as poplars. It will visit gardens to feed.

### Breeding
Nests in holes in trees, laying 2-4 white eggs, incubated for 22-24 days. Young fledge after 6-7 weeks. One, sometimes two, broods.

### When & where
Common but very locally distributed in parts of south-east England, including the west London suburbs around the River Thames and Richmond Park, and also in parts of Kent and Sussex. However, the occasional bird may be seen in many other locations in Britain, especially in south-east England. Best observed at dusk as hundreds – even thousands – of birds fly into their communal roosts.

Adult male

Juvenile

Adult female

OWLS

| J | F | M | A | M | J |
|---|---|---|---|---|---|
| J | A | S | O | N | D |

## ID FACT FILE

**SIZE**
Length 37-39cm
(14.5-15.5in).
Size of large
pigeon.

**LOOKALIKES**
Given good views
unlikely to be
mistaken for any
other species of
owl.

**VOICE**
Distinctive,
haunting, hooting
call, and piercing
'kee-wick', with
stress on second
note.

**FEEDING**
Feeds mainly on
rodents,
especially rats,
mice and voles,
but will also take
birds and
amphibians,
especially during
harsh winter
weather.

# Tawny Owl
*Strix aluco*

Our commonest and most widespread
owl, yet paradoxically one of the hardest
of its family to see, due to its almost
exclusively nocturnal lifestyle. Your best
chance of seeing one is at a winter roost,
where one or more birds will often sit in
a visible position in a hole or crevice in a
mature tree. It is one of our most
sedentary birds, rarely venturing more
than a kilometre or two away from its
home territory.

## Appearance
The Tawny Owl is best identified by its
distinctive calls: the famous hooting, and
a loud, high-pitched 'kee-wick' – giving
rise to the notion that the Tawny Owl
calls 'to-whit, to-whoo'. When you do see
one, note the classic 'owl shape', and its
medium size. If you get good views, the
plumage is dark brown (sometimes almost
grey in colour), and the species has a
typical round face, which helps it hear its
prey. It is rarely seen in flight, when it has
rounded wings and a stealthy appearance.
It hunts with great effect on silent wings,
pouncing on its unsuspecting prey.

## Behaviour
Virtually exclusively nocturnal, though
may sometimes be seen at daytime roost,
especially in autumn and winter. Highly
sedentary, rarely venturing very far from
its home territory in a wood.

OWLS

Adult

### Breeding
Nests in a hole in a tree, laying 2-5 round white eggs, which it incubates for about four weeks. Young fledge after five weeks, though often leave the nest beforehand, and may be visible nearby, huddling together on a branch of a tree like a collection of feather dusters! One brood.

### When & where
Found throughout wooded areas of Britain, including towns and suburbs, but is absent from highland areas of England and Wales, parts of north and west Scotland. Like most owls, it is not found at all in Ireland. Currently decreasing. Resident.

---

| J | F | M | A | M | J |
|---|---|---|---|---|---|
| J | A | S | O | N | D |

# Swift
*Apus apus*

### ID FACT FILE

**SIZE**
Length 16-17cm (6-6.5in).

**LOOKALIKES**
Superficially similar to Swallow and House Martin, but lacks any white in plumage.

**VOICE**
Distinctive screaming, which in the past earned the species the nickname of 'devil bird'. Calls more at dusk.

**FEEDING**
Feeds entirely on small flying insects, caught on the wing.

The ultimate flying machine, the Swift is one of the best-known summer visitors to our towns and cities. Arriving in late April or early May, Swifts announce their arrival by flying through the city skyscape, sometimes in flocks of several dozen birds, screaming as they go. It is reputed to spend many months in the air between one breeding season and the next, and if it does land on the ground, is rarely able to take off again.

### Appearance
Although superficially similar to the unrelated swallows and martins, the Swift is in fact highly distinctive. It has an all dark plumage (all British swallows and martins show some white in the plumage), cigar shaped body and narrow, swept back wings. A closer look reveals that the plumage is in fact dark brown, not black as it may first appear.

### Behaviour
Spends its entire time (apart from when feeding young or at the nest) in flight, sweeping across the sky either singly or in sociable groups. At night it flies high into the air in search of insects, which it snatches using its huge gape, and grabs brief moments of sleep on the wing.

### Breeding
Nests in roofs of buildings, laying 2-3

SWIFTS

Adults

Juvenile

white eggs, incubated for 3-4 weeks. The
young fledge after 5-8 weeks, depending on the
weather and the resulting food availability. One brood.

### When & where
Summer visitor, arriving like clockwork in late April
or the first week of May, and departing south again
in July or August. A few stragglers linger until
September. Found in towns, villages and cities
throughout Britain and Ireland, apart from the
extreme north and west. Currently in rapid decline,
possibly because of a lack of nest sites in modern
houses, or because of problems on their wintering
grounds in Africa.

| J | F | M | A | M | J |
| J | A | S | O | N | D |

## ID FACT FILE

**SIZE**
Length 16-17cm
(6-6.5in). Much
smaller than
most people
suppose – only
slightly larger
than a House
Sparrow!

**LOOKALIKES**
Absolutely none!

**VOICE**
A high-pitched
whistling call,
often uttered in
flight.

**FEEDING**
Almost
exclusively feeds
on fish and small
aquatic
invertebrates,
taken by diving
onto or beneath
the water
surface.

# Kingfisher
*Alcedo atthis*

Britain's most colourful, and arguably
most beautiful, bird is a scarce but
regular visitor to gardens, especially
those near water or with a garden pond.
It can also be found along rivers, canals
and streams, or by lakes, sometimes even
near the centre of towns and cities. If you
do suspect that a Kingfisher is taking fish
from your pond, try watching very early
in the morning, when they usually visit
gardens.

## Appearance
Dazzling electric-blue upperparts and
deep-orange underparts make it
absolutely unmistakable! It is often seen
darting away in flight. However, be aware
that Kingfishers often look much smaller
than you would expect – barely larger
than a small songbird! If you see it
perched look out for the orange on the
base of the bill – females have it but males
do not (the base of their bill is dark).

## Behaviour
Shy and retiring, Kingfishers often sit
perched quietly, and only fly at the very
last moment, dashing away up the stream
or river. They hunt by pouncing down
from a perch, plunging beneath the water
to catch tiny fish with that powerful beak.
In hard winters Kingfishers head towards
the coast, where they can still find ice-
free water to feed.

**Breeding**
Nests deep in a hole in a bank of
a river, lake or stream, where it
lays 5-7 white eggs, incubated for
19-20 days. Young fledge after 3-4
weeks, and will continue to be fed
outside the nest. Two, occasionally
three, broods.

Juvenile

**When & where**
Resident, though may move
to the coast during the winter.
Found in suitable habitats – near
rivers, lakes or streams – throughout
lowland England and Wales; scarce in
Ireland and Scotland. An occasional
visitor to gardens, whose numbers are
currently increasing.

Adult female

| J | F | M | A | M | J |
|---|---|---|---|---|---|
| J | A | S | O | N | D |

### ID FACT FILE

**Size**
Length 26-28cm (10-11in). Size of large thrush, but appears bigger, especially in flight.

**Lookalikes**
Absolutely none! Looks like giant black, white and orange-pink butterfly!

**Voice**
A distinctive, far-carrying and repetitive 'poo, poo, poo' which gives the species its name.

**Feeding**
Feeds on wide range of items including large insects and lizards.

# Hoopoe
*Upupa epops*

This gaudy and unmistakable bird is a common summer visitor throughout continental Europe, which crosses the Channel annually to Britain, usually in spring. Every few years a pair of Hoopoes stays to breed – building a nest in a hole in a tree. With the onset of global warming, it is possible that higher average summer temperatures will allow the Hoopoe to colonise southern Britain permanently as a breeding bird – a welcome addition!

### Appearance
The Hoopoe has bright, orange-pink underparts, offset by patterned black and white wings and often shows a raised crest. No other species has this combination of colours and patterns, making the Hoopoe unmistakable. In flight the black and white wings are the most obvious feature.

### Behaviour
A shy bird, often not seen as it feeds unobtrusively on the ground. Once flushed, it usually flies away, though can often be found again with careful searching. It may be detected by its distinctive and far carrying call – which gives the species its unusual English and scientific names!

### Breeding
Nests in a hole or crevice in a tree, and is often discovered by the smell produced

KINGFISHER AND HOOPOE

Adult

by its unhygienic habits. Lays
7-8 eggs, which it incubates for
15-16 days. The male then brings
food to the female and young,
which leave the nest and fly after
about four weeks. Usually one
brood, sometimes two.

## When & Where

The Hoopoe winters in Africa south of the Sahara
Desert, and is a spring and summer visitor to
much of continental Europe, being especially
common in Spain, southern France, and also in
traditionally farmed areas of eastern Europe. The
Hoopoe is an annual visitor to southern Britain,
usually arriving in March, April or May, though it
is are also found in autumn and has been known
to spend the winter here.

WOODPECKERS

| J | F | M | A | M | J |
|---|---|---|---|---|---|
| J | A | S | O | N | D |

# Wryneck
*Jynx Torquilla*

---

## ID FACT FILE

**SIZE**
Length 16-17cm
(6-6.5in). Slightly
larger than a
House Sparrow,
and appears
slimmer and
longer.

**LOOKALIKES**
Seen well, hard
to mistake for
any other bird.

**VOICE**
High-pitched,
repeated 'kee-
kee-kee', rather
like the call of a
Kestrel.

**FEEDING**
Feeds mainly on
ants taken
directly from their
nest, on a path
or lawn.

Until the Second World War the Wryneck was a fairly common and widespread British breeding bird, found in parks and gardens throughout the southern part of the country. However, sadly in the past few decades this species declined to the point of extinction here, though it still breeds commonly on the continent. If you want to see one in Britain, your best chance is to visit the east coast in spring or autumn.

## Appearance
Although a member of the woodpecker family, this bizarre-looking bird is nothing like the other European members of its tribe. From a distance it appears mainly brown or brownish-grey in colour, but if you get a closer view the plumage can be seen to be far more complex in shade and pattern. In the hand, the Wryneck reveals a unique pattern of mottling and streaking with black and grey, which resembles the bark of a tree.

## Behaviour
Like its cousin the Green Woodpecker, it spends much of its time feeding on the ground, mainly on ants. It will also perch in trees, though is fairly hard to see due to its cryptic plumage and retiring habits. If it is surprised, it will twist its neck and hiss like a snake in order to frighten off a predator!

WOODPECKERS

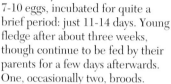

Adult

## Breeding
Breeds in a
hole in a tree,
where it lays
7-10 eggs, incubated for quite a
brief period: just 11-14 days. Young
fledge after about three weeks,
though continue to be fed by their
parents for a few days afterwards.
One, occasionally two, broods.

Adult

## When & Where
Summer visitor to Europe, found
throughout the continent (apart from Britain and
Ireland), and commonest in the east and in
Scandinavia. Scarce spring and autumn migrant to
Britain, mainly on the east coast. Some
Scandinavian birds occasionally breed in Scotland.

WOODPECKERS

| J | F | M | A | M | J |
| J | A | S | O | N | D |

## ID FACT FILE

**SIZE**
Length 31-33cm
(12-13in). Size of
Feral Pigeon.

**LOOKALIKES**
Seen well, hard
to mistake for
any other British
bird.

**VOICE**
A loud, powerful
series of high-
pitched notes,
reminiscent of a
laughing sound.

**FEEDING**
Feeds mainly on
ants, which it
sweeps up from
the ground using
a specially
adapted sticky
tongue.

# Green Woodpecker
*Picus viridis*

The largest of our three species of
woodpecker, and much bigger than its
two black and white 'spotted' relatives.
Usually seen feeding on lawns or in long
grass, and although shy, may allow quite
a close approach before it flies away. Also
may be seen climbing trees, where it
occasionally drums to attract a mate. Best
located by its laughing call, which gives
the species its country name of 'Yaffle'. It
is said to call more just before it rains,
giving it another folk name, the 'rain
bird'!

### Appearance

With its yellow-green plumage, bright-
red cap and black face mask, our largest
woodpecker is easy to identify, even on a
brief view. Also look out for its
characteristic shape, and habit of
'freezing' when first seen. Young birds
lack the black markings on the face. In
flight watch out for the heavy, pot-bellied
shape, rounded wings and undulating
flying motion.

### Behaviour

Unlike other woodpeckers, the Green
Woodpecker spends much of its time on
the ground, where it feeds on ants. It
likes large gardens with spacious lawns
and paths where there are likely to be
ants' nests, and often visits at dawn or
dusk to avoid disturbance by human

beings. It is also found in large, open parks, where it often feeds by a path and can be easily surprised as you walk or cycle by.

### Breeding
Nests in a hole in a tree which it excavates itself in early spring. Lays 5-7 white eggs, incubated for 17-19 days. Young fledge after 18-21 days. One brood.

### When & where
Found in suitable habitat (mixed woodland, parks and large gardens) throughout lowland England, Wales and southern Scotland, though due to its shy habits can be overlooked. Like all woodpeckers, it does not breed in Ireland. Populations are currently stable or increasing. Resident.

Adult male

Juvenile

WOODPECKERS

# Great Spotted Woodpecker

*Dendrocopos major*

---

## ID FACT FILE

**SIZE**
Length 22-23cm
(8.5-9in). Larger
than Starling.

**LOOKALIKES**
Superficially
resembles
Lesser Spotted,
but obviously
larger and with
distinctive
pattern.

**VOICE**
Loud, far carrying
drumming in
spring; also
distinctive,
resonant 'chip'
call.

**FEEDING**
Feeds mainly on
insects and
grubs, prised
from the surface
or beneath the
bark of a tree.

This is the larger of the two 'spotted' woodpeckers found in Britain (a third species, the Middle Spotted, is locally found on the continent of Europe). It is also by far the most numerous and widespread – any black and white woodpecker you see is almost certain to be this species. It frequently visits gardens, especially during autumn and winter, even feeding on bird tables and peanut feeders, which it may damage in an attempt to get at the contents. In spring, it has also been known to raid nest holes and nestboxes to get baby birds.

## Appearance

A medium sized woodpecker, roughly the size of a Starling. Sports an obvious contrasting black and white plumage, notably with two large oval patches on the back, which are its most distinctive field mark. Males have red on the back of the head but females lack this. Strangely, juveniles have a completely red cap, which can cause superficial confusion with males of the Lesser Spotted Woodpecker. In flight it has a distinctive undulating action.

## Behaviour

The classic woodpecker in behaviour and habits: often seen climbing up and around a branch or tree trunk, searching

WOODPECKERS

Adult male

Juvenile

for insect food, or flying
from tree to tree. An
excellent climber, using
specially adapted feet and tail.
Its distinctive call often draws
your attention to its presence high
in a tree, or as it flies overhead.

## Breeding
Nests in a specially excavated hole in a mature tree,
which it digs out in late winter or early spring, using
its powerful bill. Lays 4-7 white eggs, incubated for
16 days. Young fledge after 18-24 days. One brood.

## When & where
Found throughout England, Wales and most of
lowland Scotland, in suitable habitat such as mixed
or deciduous woodland, parks and large gardens.
Like other woodpeckers, it is completely absent from
Ireland. Currently increasing rapidly. Resident.

WOODPECKERS

# Lesser Spotted Woodpecker

*Dendrocopos minor*

## ID FACT FILE

**SIZE**
Length 14-15cm (5.5-6in). Size of House Sparrow.

**LOOKALIKES**
Like its larger cousin the Great Spotted Woodpecker, but much smaller.

**VOICE**
Quiet, gentle drumming. High-pitched, repetitive call – a weak 'kee-kee-kee-kee'.

**FEEDING**
Creeps around the trunks and branches of trees searching for small, wood boring insects and grubs, which it digs out using its sharp bill.

This is our smallest species of woodpecker, and by far the scarcest of the three species found in Britain. The Lesser Spotted Woodpecker is confined mainly to the southern part of Britain, where with careful and diligent searching it can be found in mature woodland, parks, and some gardens – though its shy and furtive habits also make it by far the hardest woodpecker to see. It does visit large, mature gardens, but is often only given away by its call or a quiet, soft, drumming sound. It rarely visits bird feeding stations.

### Appearance

If seen well, it can be told apart from its larger Great Spotted relative by its much smaller size, barred black and white back (not oval patches), and small bill. The male has red patch on forehead, while the female has a white crown. In flight, it shows the characteristic undulating action of all woodpeckers, with rounded wings.

### Behaviour

In size, appearance and behaviour, it is more like a Nuthatch or Treecreeper than other members of its family. It is most likely to be seen climbing around the trunk or branch of a mature tree. In winter it also joins tit flocks, roaming around woodlands in search of food,

where it may easily be overlooked amongst the commoner species.

**Breeding**
Nests in a hole in the branch of a tree, specially excavated by using its small but very powerful bill. The nest site is often very high up in a tall tree, making it much harder to spot than that of other woodpeckers. Lays 4-6 white eggs, incubated for 11-14 days. Young fledge after 18-21 days. One brood.

**When & where**
Found in well-managed, mature woodland all over southern Britain, though very scarce in Scotland and (like other members of the woodpecker family) completely absent from Ireland. Currently undergoing a major decline in numbers. Resident.

Adult female

Juvenile

LARKS

# Skylark
*Alauda arvensis*

## ID FACT FILE

**SIZE**
Length 18-19cm (7-7.5in).
Intermediate in size between House Sparrow and Starling.

**LOOKALIKES**
Superficially similar to other small brown birds such as Meadow Pipit.

**VOICE**
Unmistakable outpouring of rich, powerful song, which seems to go on forever.

**FEEDING**
Feeds mainly on seeds, grain and insects, mainly taken on the ground.

The Skylark is a favourite bird of the poets, immortalised by Shelley and John Clare among others. This familiar farmland species is justly celebrated for its extraordinary song, delivered high in the sky during a prolonged song flight. Once our commonest and most widespread farmland bird, Skylarks have undergone a major decline in the past few decades, due to the effects of modern farming methods on their feeding and breeding. However, in recent years attempts have been made to reverse the decline by more lark-friendly farming.

## Appearance
A large, mainly brown songbird, with paler underparts and a mottled back and wings. If seen well on the ground, it can best be identified by its bulky size and shape, and in particular by its raised crest. However, Skylarks are usually seen in flight, especially in spring and summer, when they can be easily identified by their distinctive song.

## Behaviour
On the ground it can be secretive and hard to see. Look for it in song-flight, where it may appear as a tiny speck high in the sky, seemingly hanging in the air, and moving up and down on fluttering wings as it pours out its heart in sound.

Adult

## Breeding
Breeds on the ground in arable
farmland, making a nest from
grasses in a tussock or shallow
dip, which is notoriously
impossible to find. Lays 3-5 eggs, incubated for 11
days. The young fledge after 18-20 days, but leave
the nest more than a week earlier. There may be
up to three broods in a single breeding season.

## When & Where
A farmland species, formerly found throughout
Britain in both highland and lowland habitats, but
it has suffered heavy declines in recent years. In
the original Atlas survey of Britain's breeding birds
it was our most widespread species. Resident,
though there are some local movements in autumn
and winter, when it may form large flocks.

LARKS

| J | F | M | A | M | J |
|---|---|---|---|---|---|
| J | A | S | O | N | D |

## ID FACT FILE

**SIZE**
Length 17-19cm
(6.5-7.5in).

**LOOKALIKES**
Very similar to
Skylark, though
with practice can
be told apart by
shape, field
marks and 'jizz'
(general
appearance).

**VOICE**
Varied song full
of long, fluty
notes, and
including mimicry
of many other
species.

**FEEDING**
Feeds mostly on
plant material
including seeds,
and a few
invertebrates.

# Crested Lark
*Galerida cristata*

Despite breeding commonly just across
the Channel in Calais, this continental
species has only ever been recorded in
Britain a dozen or so times, due to its
sedentary habits. However, it is a fairly
common sight on the European
mainland, sometimes seen in the most
unlikely places including car parks!
Many British birdwatchers search for it
around the hypermarkets and industrial
estates of Calais, where it breeds.

## Appearance
Superficially similar to a Skylark, but
with several distinctive field marks.
Among these is the much longer,
narrower crest, which is usually pointed
upward – though that of the Skylark can
appear almost as long at times. Other
ways to separate the two species are the
Crested Lark's greyer general
appearance, its lack of the white trailing
edge to the back of the wing, and the
buff, rather than white, outer tail
feathers. It is also identified by its
distinctive calls and song – quite
different from that of the Skylark.

## Behaviour
Like most larks, it is usually seen on the
ground, where it feeds on weed seeds, or
in flight – especially when flushed – and
can allow quite a close approach.
Outside the breeding season, in autumn

LARKS

Adult

and winter, it forms small
flocks and seeks out areas
of grass or fields where
there is plenty of food.

**Breeding**
Breeds on the ground. Lays 3-5 eggs, incubated for
11-13 days. Young leave the nest after nine days,
and fledge a few days later.

**When & Where**
Sedentary and resident throughout much of
Continental Europe including Spain and France,
where it can be found right up to the Channel
coast. Often seen on 'waste ground' by sides of
road, where few other species choose to live. Very
rare vagrant to Britain – only a handful of records,
and therefore much sought after by twitchers.

## ID FACT FILE

**SIZE**
Length 12cm
(4.75in). Slightly
smaller than its
close relative the
House Martin.

**LOOKALIKES**
Similar in size
and shape to
House Martin;
but very different
colour and
pattern.

**VOICE**
A harsh twittering
series of notes,
usually delivered
in flight.

**FEEDING**
Feeds on small
flying insects
caught on the
wing, often over
water.

# Sand Martin
*Riparia riparia*

This small brown and white hirundine (member of the swallow family) is one of the earliest spring migrants to arrive, usually coming in March or early April, and departing south to its African winter quarters in September. This may be because it feeds mainly on small insects caught over the surface of water, and there is just enough food to support it when it arrives back to our shores.

## Appearance
The Sand Martin has all brown upperparts (showing no white rump) and white underparts, with a narrow brown band across its chest. It is told apart from its close relative the House Martin by its slightly smaller size, more compact shape, and especially its colour and pattern.

## Behaviour
Although all swallows and martins sometimes feed over water, the Sand Martin is the most likely to live alongside a river, lake or stream. It builds its nest in a burrow in a sandbank, generally in a large colony numbering several dozen or more pairs. A colony can often be found by watching where feeding birds fly to, then listening for the clamour of calling birds. Sand Martins feed by flying low over the water surface in search of tiny insects.

SWALLOWS AND MARTINS

Adult

## Breeding
Breeds in the banks of rivers or gravel pits, in a burrow. Lays 4-6 eggs, incubated for 14-15 days. Young fledge after about three weeks. One or two broods.

## When & Where
Found from early spring (a few as early as mid February) to autumn, anywhere near water where there is a suitable place to nest. It often associates with other hirundines and swifts, especially where there are large concentrations of small flying insects. It can be seen in suitable habitats throughout Britain and Ireland, though may be locally scarce in places. It is currently doing quite well after major population declines in the past.

| J | F | M | A | M | J |
|---|---|---|---|---|---|
| J | A | S | O | N | D |

# Swallow
*Hirundo rustica*

## ID FACT FILE

**SIZE**
Length 17-19cm (6.5-7.5in). Larger than martins.

**LOOKALIKES**
Superficially similar to the two martins and Swift, but has distinctive shape, behaviour and field marks.

**VOICE**
Series of chattering notes, usually given in flight. Also a high-pitched 'chit'.

**FEEDING**
Feeds almost entirely on small insects, caught in its acrobatic flight using its wide gape.

Surely our most familiar and welcome summer visitor, the Swallow makes the epic five thousand mile journey to and from its winter quarters in southern Africa each spring and autumn. Once here, it is a familiar sight in most rural areas, often living alongside people in farms and villages. In recent years it has suffered population declines, possibly due to changes in farming methods which have led to there being fewer flying insects than before.

## Appearance
A slim, elegant bird, with a much longer tail than the martins or Swift. It is dark blue above, cream below, with a reddish throat. Usually seen in flight, where its elegant shape and low flying habits make it one of the most delightful birds to watch. Juveniles lack the reddish throat and appear shorter tailed than their parents.

## Behaviour
The Swallow flies low over fields, open grassy areas or water, hunting for small flying insects. In late summer and early autumn, flocks of Swallows and martins often gather on telegraph wires, chattering to each other before they head south for the winter – a good time to get really close up views.

SWALLOWS AND MARTINS

Adult male

Juvenile

## Breeding
Usually nests in old
buildings, especially
barns and old houses. It
builds a cup-shaped nest from
mud, and lays 4-5 white eggs
with reddish brown spotting, incubated for
14-16 days. Young fledge after three weeks
and often stay close to their parents for some
time after fledging. Two, sometimes three, broods.

## When & Where
A summer visitor to Britain and Europe, usually
arriving in early April and departing in September
or October; though in some mild winters birds will
begin arriving as early as February and may stay as
late as November. It is found throughout lowland
Britain and Ireland, even in the far north (including
the Northern Isles), though generally absent from
large towns and cities. Currently in decline.

| J | F | M | A | M | J |
|---|---|---|---|---|---|
| J | A | S | O | N | D |

## ID FACT FILE

**SIZE**
Length 12.5cm
(5in). Noticeably
smaller than
Swallow or Swift,
but slightly larger
than Sand Martin.

**LOOKALIKES**
Superficially
similar to Swallow
– but much more
compact.

**VOICE**
A rapid series of
high-pitched,
twittering
sounds; also a
sharp, loud
'prrrit' call.

**FEEDING**
Feeds almost
entirely on small
flying insects,
caught on the
wing.

# House Martin
*Delichon urbica*

One of the classic birds of urban and
suburban Britain, the House Martin is a
familiar sight throughout the spring and
summer, as flocks fly over our villages,
towns and cities, giving their characteristic
twittering calls. It depends on humans
for nesting sites, as its name suggests!
Before man built houses to live in, the
House Martin nested in the openings of
caves and on cliff faces and a few still do
so along our coasts.

## Appearance
Given good views, it can easily be told
apart from its close relative the Swallow
(and the unrelated Swift) by its smaller
size, more compact shape, shallowly forked
tail, and white rump. Upperparts are dark,
bluish-black; underparts are white, giving a
more contrasting appearance than its
relatives. The closely related Sand Martin
is much browner in tone, and lacks the
House Martin's white rump.

## Behaviour
Generally seen in flight, hawking for
insect food over houses. When breeding,
it may be seen collecting tiny balls of
mud to build its nest. Like Swallows,
House Martins often gather on telegraph
wires in late summer and autumn,
twittering away to each other, in
preparation for their long migratory
journey south to Africa.

SWALLOWS AND MARTINS

Adult

Adult
(from
below)

## Breeding
Builds a characteristic
cup-shaped nest out of
tiny balls of mud,
usually under the eaves of houses –
generally forming a colony of anything
between three and a dozen or more breeding pairs –
but will also use artificial nestboxes. Lays 3-5 whitish
eggs, incubated for 14-16 days. Young fledge after
2-3 weeks. Two, sometimes three, broods.

## When & where
A summer visitor, arriving mid-April and departing
in September. It is found throughout lowland
Britain and Ireland, apart from the extreme north
and west. Currently declining, possibly as a result of
shortage of mud to build nests, though also because
of drought in their African winter quarters.

PIPITS

| J | F | M | A | M | J |
| J | A | S | O | N | D |

## ID FACT FILE

**SIZE**
Length 14.5cm
(5.75in). Size of
House Sparrow,
but slimmer.

**LOOKALIKES**
Superficially
resembles
several small
brown birds,
such as Linnet
and Skylark.

**VOICE**
Call a thin 'seep',
often given in
flight; song a
jumbled series of
notes often
delivered in
parachuting song
flight.

**FEEDING**
Feeds mainly on
insects, and also
takes seeds in
autumn and
winter.

# Meadow Pipit
*Anthus pratensis*

The classic lbj – 'little brown job' – of
birdwatching lore. The Meadow Pipit is
common and widespread throughout
upland and lowland habitats across most
of Britain. Often neglected by
birdwatchers as a result, a closer look
reveals that the Meadow Pipit is in fact
an attractive little bird, characteristic of
rural and agricultural parts of the
country.

## Appearance
A small, slim songbird, about the size of
a sparrow, with a streaked brown
plumage and thin bill (which helps tell it
apart from sparrows, finches and larks –
all of which have a thicker, stubby bill).
It often manages to remain hidden until
flushed, when it can best be identified
by its thin, single note call.

## Behaviour
Unobtrusive except when males
perform their extraordinary song flight
during the breeding season: flying up
from the ground or a song post, then
parachuting down to the ground
(sometimes from a great height), singing
as they go. In autumn and winter
Meadow Pipits gather in small flocks on
open ground, where they feed on seeds
rather than their spring and summer
diet of insects.

Adult

### Breeding

It builds a shallow, unobtrusive, cup-shaped nest from grasses, on the ground, which, like the nest of the Skylark, can be very hard to find. There it lays 3-5 eggs, incubated for 13 days. Young fledge after 10-14 days. Usually two broods.

### When & Where

Resident, found throughout Britain and Ireland in most habitats. One of the most widespread species in the country, due to its ability to thrive in a variety of different places; though rarely found in the centre of cities. Often heard or seen overhead during autumn migration, when flocks of birds may undertake local movements, especially in response to cold weather.

| J | F | M | A | M | J |
|---|---|---|---|---|---|
| J | A | S | O | N | D |

## ID FACT FILE

**SIZE**
Length 17cm
(6.5in). Our
smallest wagtail,
slightly longer
than a House
Sparrow.

**LOOKALIKES**
Can easily be
mistaken for
Grey Wagtail,
which is longer
and has grey and
black in the
plumage.

**VOICE**
Call a long,
drawn out
'tsweep'.

**FEEDING**
Feeds on small
insects picked
up from ground
or by flycatching.

# Yellow Wagtail
*Motacilla flava*

One of our most attractive and delicate birds, the Yellow Wagtail is purely a summer visitor to Britain and Europe – so any 'yellow' wagtail seen in winter is not this species but its close cousin the Grey Wagtail. In recent years this beautiful species has declined in numbers, due to the draining of marshy areas and wet meadows in the countryside. Nowadays it is most likely to be seen on bird reserves.

## Appearance
A slim, slender looking bird – obviously a wagtail from its stance and habits. It is bright yellow below, olive green above, with the characteristic long tail of its family. Told apart from the Grey Wagtail by its slightly smaller size, shorter tail, and lack of grey or black in its plumage. The male is brighter yellow than the female. Juveniles can appear quite greyish in colour, and can be mistaken for young Pied Wagtails. In flight its slender shape and long tail are noticeable.

## Behaviour
Yellow Wagtails usually prefer to breed in damp, muddy areas such as wet meadows and marshes, especially around livestock where insects are common. On migration they are often seen around the edge of lakes and

WAGTAILS

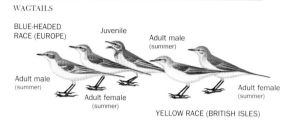

BLUE-HEADED RACE (EUROPE)

Juvenile

Adult male (summer)

Adult male (summer)

Adult female (summer)

Adult female (summer)

YELLOW RACE (BRITISH ISLES)

other marshy areas, or even perched on fence posts and barbed wire fences, especially in traditional farming areas.

## Breeding
Nests in a shallow scrape on the ground, where it builds a cup-shaped nest out of grasses, and lined with wool or hair from farm animals. Lays 4-6 eggs, incubated for 12 days or so. The young leave the nest after 11-12 days and fly a few days later. One, sometimes two, broods.

## When & Where
A summer visitor, arriving in mid to late April and departing south to Africa in August or September. Mainly found in eastern, central and southern England; a few in Wales. Currently decreasing in population and range.

WAGTAILS

| J | F | M | A | M | J |
| J | A | S | O | N | D |

## ID FACT FILE

**SIZE**
Length 18-19cm
(7-7.5in). Our
largest wagtail.

**LOOKALIKES**
Superficially like
Yellow Wagtail;
but black or grey
in plumage
distinctive.

**VOICE**
A loud, piercing
two-note call,
similar to Pied
Wagtail's, but
sharper and
more metallic in
sound.

**FEEDING**
Feeds almost
entirely on
insects, but will
also take tiny
aquatic
invertebrates and
small fish.

# Grey Wagtail
*Motacilla cinerea*

This elegant bird surely deserves a better
name – perhaps 'lemon-bellied wagtail' –
to reflect its colourful and attractive
appearance. Generally at home on fast
flowing streams and rivers, where it sits
on rocks and catches insects, it may also
be seen in gardens and parks, especially
near water. Like other water-loving
songbirds such as the Dipper, it also bobs
up and down while feeding in a
characteristic manner – a good way to
spot it at a distance.

## Appearance
More elegant and slightly slimmer in
appearance than the commoner Pied and
Yellow Wagtails. Adults have steel-grey
upperparts and lemon-yellow underparts,
though the male shows more yellow than
the female, whose breast and belly can
appear mostly white. It can be told apart
from the similar Yellow Wagtail (a
summer visitor) by its shape and colour
pattern. In breeding season males have a
black throat, which in winter turns white.
In flight, it appears very long and slim,
with a bounding flight action. Juveniles
are greyish in appearance, but usually
show some yellow under the tail.

## Behaviour
Like all wagtails, it has a characteristic
gait and stance, wagging its long, slender
tail up and down as it walks or even when

WAGTAILS

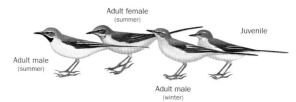

Adult female
(summer)

Juvenile

Adult male
(summer)

Adult male
(winter)

it is stood still. Usually seen by or very near water, hunting for food amongst the shallows or on stones or rocks. Flies low over water, often calling, which is a good indication of its presence.

## Breeding
Nests very near a river or stream, usually building a nest in a hole, crack or crevice inside a wall or stone bridge. Lays 4-6 buff, spotted eggs, incubated for 11-14 days. Young leave the nest after two weeks or so. Two, sometimes three, broods.

## When & where
Found in suitable habitat throughout lowland Britain and Ireland, though rare or absent from parts of eastern England. Currently on the increase. Resident.

# Pied/White Wagtail
*Motacilla alba*

Our commonest and most familiar
wagtail, this attractive little bird is a
regular and frequent sight in most of our
towns, parks and gardens. It can often be
seen searching for its tiny insect food
along a pavement or a grassy verge, and
is equally at home feeding on open
lawns.  It is often heard as it calls from a
rooftop or as it flies overhead – listen out
for the distinctive two note call.

## Appearance
The only long-tailed, small, black and
white bird found in Britain or northern
Europe, the Pied Wagtail is black and
grey above and white below, with a black
throat. Females appear greyer than
males, while juveniles can look brown in
colour. In flight, its long tail and
bounding pattern are very distinctive. On
the continent there is a different race,
known as the White Wagtail, which has a
much paler back contrasting with the
dark cap.

## Behaviour
Usually seen walking back and forth
across a pavement or short grassy lawn
while looking for tiny morsels of food,
which it picks up with its slender beak. It
will also perch on roofs, wagging its tail
for balance. It is very sociable, especially
in winter, when several dozen (or even
several hundred) birds may gather in

## ID FACT FILE
**SIZE**
Length 18cm
(7in). Slightly
longer than a
House Sparrow.
**LOOKALIKES**
Pretty
unmistakable;
though juvenile
Grey and Yellow
Wagtails can
resemble the
young of this
species.
**VOICE**
A loud,
distinctive two
note call, usually
written 'chis-ick',
with the
emphasis on the
second syllable.
**FEEDING**
Feeds mainly on
tiny insects and
other
invertebrates,
picked up in its
sharp, pointed
bill.

| J | F | M | A | M | J |
| J | A | S | O | N | D |

WAGTAILS

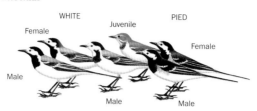

town and city centres to roost for warmth – an incredible sight and sound often overlooked by people hurrying home!

## Breeding
Nests in holes in walls, building a small nest lined with hair and feathers. Lays 5-6 pale eggs finely spotted darker, incubated for 11-16 days. Young fledge after just 11-16 days. Two or three broods.

## When & where
Found throughout Britain and Ireland, apart from the extreme uplands. It is common in our towns, suburbs and cities and the population is currently stable – Pied Wagtails appear to have adapted well to living alongside human beings. Resident.

| J | F | M | A | M | J |
|---|---|---|---|---|---|
| J | A | S | O | N | D |

## ID FACT FILE

**SIZE**
Length 18cm (7in). Slightly smaller than Starling.

**LOOKALIKES**
No other bird has this combination of appearance and habits.

**VOICE**
A quiet, delicate trilling call, often uttered by several birds at once.

**FEEDING**
In winter, prefers berries, which the birds will strip from a tree or bush. May also 'flycatch' for insects, especially in mild weather.

# Waxwing
*Bombycilla garrulous*

One of our rarest and most distinctive town and garden birds, the Waxwing is in fact an irregular visitor to Britain, whose arrival in autumn is governed by food supplies in its sub-Arctic home. Some years see many thousands of Waxwings arriving in autumn – most on the east coast – in other years there are virtually none. Arrivals spend the winter feeding avidly on berry bushes, sometimes in gardens or parks, before returning north in spring.

## Appearance
Given good views, the Waxwing is hard to confuse with any other bird. However, in flight and in a flock they can resemble Starlings. In fact the Waxwing is slightly smaller and plumper, with delicate brown plumage, a raised crest, and red and yellow markings on the wings that give the species its name.

## Behaviour
Waxwings are very sociable, usually seen in flocks of up to several dozen birds which travel together in search of food. Once they arrive in a particular area they will strip a berry bush bare, then depart within a day or two in search of more food. For this reason they usually attract the attention of householders, who face the prospect of having

birdwatchers peering into their garden to catch sight of these splendid birds!

**Breeding**
The Waxwing does not breed in Britain or Ireland – its home range is in sub-Arctic Scandinavia and Russia. Here, it builds a cup-shaped nest out of twigs and grass, and lays 5-6 eggs, incubated for two weeks. The young fledge 2-3 weeks later.

**When & where**
Autumn and winter visitor, arriving in October or November and departing back to Scandinavia and Russia in March or April. May be seen almost anywhere, but commonest in coastal eastern counties of England and Scotland. During 'irruption years' there may be many thousands of Waxwings in the country.

Adult

Juvenile

WREN AND DUNNOCK

| J | F | M | A | M | J |
| J | A | S | O | N | D |

# Wren
*Troglodytes troglodytes*

## ID FACT FILE

**SIZE**
Length 9-10cm (3.5-4in). One of our smallest birds.

**LOOKALIKES**
Seen well, cannot be confused with any other species.

**VOICE**
Extraordinarily loud and piercing song: full of trills and ending with a rapid series of notes. Call a loud 'tic'.

**FEEDING**
Feeds on small insects and other invertebrates, found by foraging in the spaces between rocks or stones.

Despite being our commonest breeding bird, with over ten million breeding pairs in Britain and Ireland, the Wren is not as well known as some other species because of its skulking habits and small size. Yet it lives in most gardens, being able to adapt to a wide variety of habitats – whether urban, suburban or rural. In the past the Wren suffered very badly from hard winters, its population often declining as a result. The recent run of very mild winters has helped it maintain and increase its numbers.

## Appearance
The Wren is the only small bird which habitually cocks its tail. Tiny, russet brown above, paler buff-brown below, with barring on the flanks and a short pale stripe behind the eye. Most often heard before it is seen – its trilling song is one of the loudest of any songbird, and can be heard from very early in the New Year, especially in milder parts of southern Britain.

## Behaviour
Often skulks around unobtrusively, hopping about in a rockery or the base of a shrubbery in search of tiny morsels of food. Rarely seen in flight – but if you do catch a glimpse of one, the tiny whirring wings are very distinctive.

WREN AND DUNNOCK

Adult

Juvenile

## Breeding

Builds a hidden, dome-shaped nest, out of moss, grass and leaves, often in a garden. In fact the male will build half a dozen or more 'cock's nests' in order for the female to choose the best! Lays 5-8 whitish eggs, incubated for 12-20 days. Young fledge after 2-3 weeks. Two broods.

## When & where

Found throughout Britain and Ireland, in almost all habitats including rocky islands and sea-cliffs as well as parks and gardens. For such a small bird it is extraordinarily resilient and adaptable. Numbers are currently increasing as a result of very mild winters. Resident.

| J | F | M | A | M | J |
|---|---|---|---|---|---|
| J | A | S | O | N | D |

## ID FACT FILE

**SIZE**
Length 14.5cm
(5.75in). About
the size of a
House Sparrow.

**LOOKALIKES**
Superficially
resembles a
female House
Sparrow.

**VOICE**
Rather
monotonous
song; a soft
warble with no
clear beginning
or end.

**FEEDING**
Feeds mainly on
small insects
and other
invertebrates,
picked up from
the ground,
though will also
take seeds,
especially in
winter.

# Dunnock
*Prunella modularis*

Often overlooked, and frequently
mistaken for a female House Sparrow,
the Dunnock is in fact one of our
commonest and most fascinating garden
birds. It also has an amazing sex life –
with all kinds of strategies played out by
rival males and females! Males breed
with several females; but the females
themselves will often seek out other
males. Once known as the 'hedge
sparrow', in fact it is a member of the
accentor family – a group of mountain-
dwelling birds found in Europe and Asia.

## Appearance

Superficially sparrow-like, though a
closer look reveals that its shape is in fact
more like that of a Robin. If seen well,
the purplish grey head, face and throat,
contrasting with a reddish brown back,
are very distinctive. The Dunnock's
posture is also rather more horizontal,
like a Robin; whereas other ground-
feeding garden birds tend to 'stand up'
more. Juveniles are streakier below, and
less colourful.

## Behaviour

A shy, retiring bird, often found deep in a
shrubbery or at the edge of a flower-bed,
where it can be hard to see well. Early on
in the breeding season males become
much more active and noticeable, often
singing their rather nondescript song from

WREN AND DUNNOCK

Fresh Adult

Worn Adult

Juvenile

a fence post or high on a bush or shrub. Males can also sometimes be seen chasing each other around the garden, as they pursue several females at once.

## Breeding
Builds a cup-shaped nest in dense foliage, from twigs and grass lined with hair and feathers. Lays 4-6 sky-blue eggs, incubated for 12-13 days. Young fledge after 11-12 days. Two, sometimes three, broods.

## When & where
Resident. Found throughout Britain and Ireland apart from the extreme north and west, and the highlands and islands. Currently declining in numbers.

THRUSHES AND CHATS

| J | F | M | A | M | J |
|---|---|---|---|---|---|
| J | A | S | O | N | D |

## ID FACT FILE

**SIZE**
Length 14cm
(5.5in). A little
smaller than a
House Sparrow.

**LOOKALIKES**
Adults
unmistakable;
juvenile may
cause some
confusion.

**VOICE**
Beautiful,
plaintive song;
sung in sweet
phrases. Robins
sing all year
round as they
defend autumn
and winter
territories.
Variety of calls
including sharp
'tic'.

**FEEDING**
Generally
insectivorous,
but also feeds
on seeds,
especially in
winter. Loves
mealworms!

# Robin
*Erithacus rubecula*

Britain's favourite garden bird is also one
of our most familiar: loved by gardeners
and householders everywhere for its
confiding habits. Originally a woodland
species, the Robin has adapted well to
living alongside human beings, and is
welcome in any garden. To attract them,
try digging your flower beds or bribing
them with tasty mealworms! Incidentally,
the association of this species with
Christmas cards is because the early
Victorian postmen wore red uniforms, so
were given the nickname 'robins'!

## Appearance
An adult robin, with its orange-red breast
and throat, brown upperparts bordered
with grey, and black beady eye, is
unmistakable. The juvenile is roughly the
same shape as the adult but has a very
different, speckled plumage, lacking any
red tones, for camouflage after leaving
the nest.

## Behaviour
Generally seen hopping about on the
lawn, on rockeries, or in undergrowth,
where it searches for insect food. It will
also come to bird tables, and seed and
nut feeders. Some birds will even feed
from the hand. It is much more tame in
Britain than on the continent, where it
tends to be a shy woodland bird. Unlike
most British birds, the Robin defends its

THRUSHES AND CHATS

Adult

Juvenile

territories throughout the year, so it is not at all unusual to hear one singing in autumn or winter. It also often sings at night, leading some people to confuse this species with the Nightingale.

**Breeding**
An early breeder, building a cup-shaped nest in a shrub or bush, or sometimes in unusual sites such as lavatory cisterns. It will use open-fronted nestboxes and lays 5-7 bluish-white eggs, incubated for 12-14 days. Young fledge after 12-15 days. Two, sometimes three, broods.

**When & Where**
Resident, with immigrants from Europe in autumn & winter. Found throughout Britain & Ireland. Common and currently thriving.

THRUSHES AND CHATS

| J | F | M | A | M | J |
|---|---|---|---|---|---|
| J | A | S | O | N | D |

# Nightingale
*Luscinia megarhynchos*

### ID FACT FILE

**Size**
Length 16.5cm
(6.5in). Larger
and bulkier than
the Robin, with a
longer tail.

**Lookalikes**
If seen well, hard
to confuse with
anything else.

**Voice**
A stunning and
varied collection
of remarkable
sounds – must
be heard to be
appreciated!

**Feeding**
Feeds on
invertebrates
caught by
foraging through
leaf litter on
ground.

This legendary songster, celebrated by
poets from Keats and Clare to Ted
Hughes, really does live up to its billing,
delivering an extraordinary series of
complex notes, tunes and rhythms.
Although males mainly sing at night,
when they have few rivals, they do also
sing by day – especially early in the
breeding season when they are trying to
attract a mate. Like many birds with
beautiful songs, the bird's plumage is
relatively drab.

## Appearance
Nightingales are hardly ever seen – even
when you watch and wait for a long time
– so are usually best identified by their
song: which must be heard and
experienced to be appreciated. If you do
catch a glimpse of this shy songster, you
will see an anonymous looking brown
bird, larger than a Robin, with few
distinctive field markings apart from its
brighter rufous tail, which is in marked
contrast to the rest of the plumage. The
tail is often cocked distinctively.

## Behaviour
Once they arrive back from their African
winter quarters, Nightingales are
occasionally fairly visible for a day or two,
sometimes even singing out in full view
at the base of a bush or tree. After this
they revert to their usual habit of

THRUSHES AND CHATS

Adult

Juvenile

skulking deep
inside the centre
of a bush to
deliver its amazing song (which can
continue throughout the night).

## Breeding
Breeds in dense foliage in scrub or woodland. It
builds a nest out of grass and leaves near or even
on the ground, where it lays 4-5 eggs, incubated for
13 days or so. Young fledge after about 11 days.

## When & Where
Summer visitor, widespread in southern and
western Europe. Widespread but localised in
southern Britain, usually in woods or by sandy
heaths, where there is plenty of dense scrub. In
recent years it has declined and even disappeared
from many areas.

THRUSHES AND CHATS

| J | F | M | A | M | J |
|---|---|---|---|---|---|
| J | A | S | O | N | D |

## ID FACT FILE

**SIZE**
Length 14.5cm
(5.75in). Roughly
the size of a
House Sparrow.

**LOOKALIKES**
Females can be
confused with
Common
Redstart, though
habitat usually
very different.
Males more or
less
unmistakable!

**VOICE**
Quiet, fairly rapid
warble,
reminiscent of
ball bearings
being clattered
together.

**FEEDING**
Feeds on small
invertebrates and
some fruit.

# Black Redstart
*Phoenicurus ochruros*

In Britain this species is generally confined to industrial sites and the urban jungle, being found breeding in the most unlikely locations – including nuclear power stations, on city skyscrapers and on busy building sites. However, in the rest of Europe the Black Redstart is most likely to be seen on rocky hillsides. The species colonised Britain in the years between the two world wars, but numbers really took off after the Second World War, when it took advantage of bomb sites to breed.

### Appearance
Robin-like in size and habits, but slimmer in build, with a longer tail. Males in breeding plumage are all black with a rufous tail, slightly less bright in winter. Females are a greyish brown, also showing rufous on tail – a very distinctive field mark. Females and juveniles are darker and greyer in tone than the Common Redstart.

### Behaviour
Male often sings from a high building or perched on industrial machinery, though its song can sometimes be hard to distinguish above the city noise. On the continent this species is more likely to perch on rocks or cliffs. In winter it may be found on other sites such as

THRUSHES AND CHATS

Adult male    Adult femaie    Juvenile    Adult female

cliffs or rocky shores, where it hops about
looking for insects to eat.

## Breeding
Breeds in a hole on a wall or the side of a
building. Builds a nest from grass and leaves
and lays 4-6 eggs incubated for 14-17 days.
Young fledge after 12-20 days, though parents
continue to care for them for another 2-3
weeks. Usually two, occasionally three, broods.

## When & Where
A partial migrant, often wintering at lower
altitudes or near coasts. Common throughout
continental Europe, with a few pairs breeding
in southern Britain including some in central
London!

| J | F | M | A | M | J |
| J | A | S | O | N | D |

# Blackbird

*Turdus merula*

This member of the thrush family is one of the most familiar British and European birds, as its name suggests. Originally a woodland species, it has adapted very well to nesting and feeding in towns and gardens, though it still seems wary of humans. It is famed for its glorious song, often delivered from high on a rooftop or from the top of a tree, where it can be heard for some distance around.

## ID FACT FILE

**SIZE**
Length 24-25cm (9.5-10in). Medium sized to large thrush.

**LOOKALIKES**
Female superficially resembles thrushes, but lacks spotted breast.

**VOICE**
Distinctive, tuneful song, with rich tone and clear phrases. Variety of calls, such as the chattering alarm when flushed.

**FEEDING**
Feeds mainly on earthworms and other invertebrates, dug up from lawns and flower beds.

## Appearance

The male lives up to his name: having an all-black plumage with a bright yellow bill. However, Blackbirds are particularly prone to albino markings on their plumage – occasionally an all white specimen is found! The female is mid-brown in colour, with some pale streaking on the throat and breast. Juveniles are speckled, and can be mistaken for a Song or Mistle Thrush at first sight, though lack the same clear breast markings.

## Behaviour

A confident bird, often feeding in the open on lawns, where it pulls up worms with that powerful beak. Territorially aggressive, the males will chase each other off, especially during the spring, uttering a rattling alarm call as they go. In winter it may be more inclined to feed

THRUSHES AND CHATS

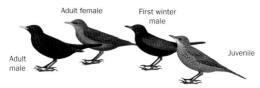

Adult female   First winter male

Adult male   Juvenile

alongside other birds, often eating apples and other windfall fruit from beneath trees.

## Breeding

Builds a neat, cup-shaped nest of grasses lined with mud, usually in a bush or shrub. Lays 3-5 greenish eggs spotted with reddish brown, incubated for 12-15 days, and young fledge after 12-15 days. There may be up to five broods in a single season – helped by the fact that they begin nesting very early in the year, sometimes when frost or snow is still on the ground.

## When & where

Found throughout Britain and Ireland, apart from highland areas. Common, but has recently undergone decline. Resident.

THRUSHES AND CHATS

| J | F | M | A | M | J |
|---|---|---|---|---|---|
| J | A | S | O | N | D |

## ID FACT FILE

**SIZE**
Length 25.5cm (10in). A large thrush.

**LOOKALIKES**
Similar to Mistle thrush, but much more colourful and slightly less bulky.

**VOICE**
A loud, harsh and repetitive 'chack' call, often given in flight.

**FEEDING**
Feeds mainly on fruit and berries, taken either from the bush or as windfall from the ground.

# Fieldfare
*Turdus pilaris*

This large thrush is almost exclusively a winter visitor to Britain, arriving in autumn and staying until spring, before it heads north and east to breed. On the continent of Europe it is one of the commonest breeding birds, especially in Scandinavia. It is usually found on farmland or along hedgerows, often in the company of other thrushes such as the Redwing. However, it will also visit gardens to feed, especially during periods of harsh winter weather when ice and snow make food scarce elsewhere.

## Appearance
Almost as big as a Mistle Thrush, and superficially similar, but a close look reveals that the Fieldfare is much more colourful, with a bright-yellow bill, grey head, russet upperparts and pale yellow underparts streaked with black. In undulating flight it appears pot-bellied, long-tailed and bulky, its grey rump contrasting with its darker tail and wings.

## Behaviour
A noisy, sociable bird, which often forms large flocks to feed, either in bushes or on the ground. Like other thrushes it will sometimes defend a particular bush against intruders. It is often seen flying lazily overhead or feeding in a bush, chattering as it does so.

THRUSHES AND CHATS

Adult

Juvenile

### Breeding

Breeds mainly in Scandinavia, and
eastern Europe and Russia, though a
few pairs breed annually in northern
and eastern Britain, especially
Scotland. It builds a cup-shaped
nest in the fork of a tree, and lays 5-6 eggs,
incubated for 10-13 days. The young leave the nest
after about two weeks. One, sometimes two, broods.

Adult

### When & where

An autumn and winter visitor to most areas of Britain
and Ireland, though commoner in the milder south
and east of the country. Not as common in towns as
other members of its family, but will visit gardens
during harsh winter weather. Numbers vary from year
to year, depending on breeding success in home range.

THRUSHES AND CHATS

| J | F | M | A | M | J |
|---|---|---|---|---|---|
| J | A | S | O | N | D |

## ID FACT FILE

**SIZE**
Length 23cm
(9in). Slightly
larger than the
Starling.

**LOOKALIKES**
Similar to Mistle
Thrush, but
smaller; also can
be confused with
Redwing.

**VOICE**
Rich, tuneful and
melodic song,
with clear groups
of phrases,
usually in threes.

**FEEDING**
Feeds mainly on
earthworms,
slugs and snails,
so very popular
amongst
gardeners as a
means of natural
pest control!

# Song Thrush
*Turdus philomelos*

One of our best-loved garden birds, the
Song Thrush has recently suffered a
major and very sudden population
decline, its numbers dropping by well
over 50 per cent in many areas. This is
almost certainly due to lack of food
caused by modern farming methods,
which do not encourage enough insects.
What was once the classic 'sound of the
suburbs' has now fallen silent in some
areas, though it is still found in many
parks and gardens, especially in leafy
areas where there are large trees.

## Appearance
A small, neat thrush, with a mid-brown
back, pale, buffish-yellow underparts
spotted with blackish-brown – the spots
are smaller and more heart-shaped than
that of its larger cousin the Mistle
Thrush. As you might expect from its
name, the song is also very distinctive: a
repeated series of phrases, usually in
groups of three, in the mid range – not as
deep as the Blackbird but lower in pitch
than the Robin.

## Behaviour
In early spring, it perches on a roof or
tree to herald the new season with its
lovely song. Otherwise it is often
unobtrusive and quite hard to see as it
forages for food in shrubberies, flower
beds and on lawns.

THRUSHES AND CHATS

Adult

Adult

## Breeding

Builds a neat, cup-shaped nest lined with mud, in a bush or shrub. It lays 3-5 sky blue eggs speckled with tiny black spots, incubated for 12-14 days. Young fledge after 12-15 days.

Juvenile

Song Thrushes often start breeding very early in the year, especially if there has been a mild winter. Two, sometimes three, broods.

## When & Where

Resident, though there are some immigrants from Europe in the winter. Found throughout Britain and Ireland, apart from upland areas of Scotland and relies heavily on gardens for places to nest and feed.

| J | F | M | A | M | J |
|---|---|---|---|---|---|
| J | A | S | O | N | D |

# Redwing
*Turdus iliacus*

## ID FACT FILE

**SIZE**
Length 21cm (8in). Our smallest thrush; size of Starling.

**LOOKALIKES**
Song Thrush; but much darker and with key field marks.

**VOICE**
A thin, high-pitched call, generally given in flight.

**FEEDING**
Feeds mainly on berries, either taken direct from a bush or from the ground. Like other thrushes, is also partial to windfall fruit, especially apples.

Our smallest thrush is primarily an autumn and winter visitor to Britain and Ireland, though a few pairs do stay to breed, virtually all in northern Scotland. Like its larger cousin the Fieldfare, the Redwing often gathers in flocks to seek out food: notably berries on bushes. It is more likely to visit gardens than the Fieldfare, especially during spells of cold weather when food can be scarce.

## Appearance
The Redwing is slightly smaller than the Song Thrush, and much darker in overall appearance. Surprisingly, the orangey-red patch on the flanks that gives the species its name is not always the first thing you notice – the creamy eye-stripe is often a better identification feature, especially when seen at a distance. In flight it appears broad-winged and short-tailed; with a distinctive flight silhouette. It often calls when on migration – a thin, high-pitched note.

## Behaviour
A sociable bird, generally seen in small groups or larger flocks, often along with other members of the thrush family. It will frequently come to gardens to feed, especially those near open fields. Listen out for migrating Redwings during clear autumn nights as they pass overhead, often in quite large flocks.

THRUSHES AND CHATS

Adult    Juvenile

Adult

## Breeding

A rare breeder in Britain, mostly in
the north of England or Scotland,
and unlikely to do so in gardens or
towns. It builds a cup-shaped nest in a tree or
sometimes on the ground. Lays 4-6 eggs for 12-13
days; young fledge after about two weeks. Generally
manages two broods.

## When & where

An autumn and winter visitor, arriving in October
and November and departing northwards to breed
in March or April. Common and widespread
throughout Britain and Ireland, especially in rural
areas, and is also seen on playing fields, especially
early in the morning or after a spell of rain.

| J | F | M | A | M | J |
|---|---|---|---|---|---|
| J | A | S | O | N | D |

## ID FACT FILE

**Size**
Length 27cm
(10.5in). Our
largest thrush.

**Lookalikes**
Song Thrush
(much smaller)
and Fieldfare
(more colourful).

**Voice**
Song like a cross
between a Song
Thrush and
Blackbird, with
the repetition of
the former and
rich tone of the
latter. Harsh
rattling call,
usually given in
flight.

**Feeding**
In spring and
summer feeds
mainly on
earthworms and
other
invertebrates,
taken from the
soil or ground. In
autumn and
winter prefers
fruit and berries.

# Mistle Thrush
*Turdus viscivorus*

Our largest thrush, almost the size and
bulk of a pigeon, the Mistle Thrush is
named for its love of the berries of the
Mistletoe, though like other members of
its family it is partial to all berries and
fruits. Like many other woodland and
farmland birds it has undergone major
declines in recent years; though it
continues to thrive in open parkland with
plenty of scattered mature trees which it
uses as song posts. The decline is perhaps
due to a lack of food; once again as a
result of modern farming methods.
Mistle Thrushes generally only visit large
gardens in rural or suburban parts of the
country.

**Appearance**
It is much larger and noticeably paler in
appearance than the Song Thrush, with
greyish-brown upperparts, and pale
underparts thickly spotted with black. In
flight, its pale underwings and large size
are obvious. It can be told apart from the
similar sized Fieldfare by lack of colour
on its head, back and underparts,
especially if you get close views.

**Behaviour**
In summer, males often sit high on a
prominent tree, delivering their
characteristic song: like a cross between a
Blackbird (in tone) and a Song Thrush
(in rhythm). In autumn and winter, Mistle

THRUSHES AND CHATS

Adult          Juvenile          Adult

Thrushes gather together in large
flocks, often chattering as they fly
overhead – the rattling sound is very noticeable once
learned. It will also defend berry bushes against all
comers: including members of its own species.

### Breeding
Builds a large nest, usually in the fork of a mature
tree, and lays 3-5 greenish-blue eggs, with light-
brown speckling, which are incubated for 12-15
days. Young fledge after 12-16 days. Two,
occasionally three, broods.

### When & where
Common and widespread in parks and large gardens
throughout Britain and Ireland where it is resident.

WARBLERS

| J | F | M | A | M | J |
|---|---|---|---|---|---|
| J | A | S | O | N | D |

## ID FACT FILE

**SIZE**
Length 14cm (5.5in). Large, long-tailed warbler; about the size of a Great Tit but slimmer.

**LOOKALIKES**
Lesser Whitethroat is similar but greyer, and even harder to see!

**VOICE**
A variety of vocalisations, including a fast, chattering warble and several harsh calls.

**FEEDING**
Feeds mainly on small insects, caught in flight or taken from vegetation.

# Whitethroat
*Sylvia communis*

Although often overlooked, this little warbler is in fact one of our commonest and most widespread summer visitors, widely found in suitable scrubby habitats throughout the whole of Britain and Ireland, apart from the extreme highlands and islands. Over 30 years ago the species suffered a major crash in numbers due to drought in the Sahel Zone of western Africa, losing up to 90 per cent of the British population. However, since then it has bounced back and is currently doing well – though it may be affected by loss of habitat as a result of global warming.

## Appearance
A slender, brightly-coloured warbler, with a noticeably long tail, often held cocked. Males have a chestnut-brown back and wings, grey head and a prominent white throat, which is puffed out when singing. Females are slightly duller than males, but with a similar overall pattern. In flight the Whitethroat appears very slim and long tailed.

## Behaviour
A skulking bird that often hides deep in a bush or scrubby plant, only showing itself occasionally. In spring, however, singing males will sit up on a bush or launch themselves into the air on a parachuting song flight! It is best searched for on calm, sunny days in May or June.

WARBLERS

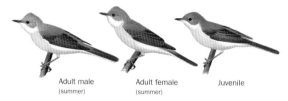

Adult male
(summer)

Adult female
(summer)

Juvenile

**Breeding**
Builds a cup-shaped nest, hidden low in bushes
such as brambles, and lays 4-5 buffish-white eggs
with darker spots, incubated for 11-13 days. Young
fledge after 10-12 days. One, often two, broods.

**When & Where**
A summer visitor, arriving in April and leaving in
September for its winter quarters in sub-Saharan
Africa. Common and widespread in suitable
habitats throughout England and Wales; more
thinly spread in Scotland and Ireland, and absent
from the far north.

WARBLERS

| J | F | M | A | M | J |
|---|---|---|---|---|---|
| J | A | S | O | N | D |

## ID FACT FILE

**SIZE**
Length 14cm
(5.5in). A
medium to large
warbler.

**LOOKALIKES**
Blackcap (but
note black or
brown cap) and
Chiffchaff, which
also has dark
legs but is
greener in tone,
and smaller.

**VOICE**
Song very easily
confused with
that of the
Blackcap, its
close relative.
With practice, can
be told apart by
faster pace and
less fluty tone.

**FEEDING**
Feeds mainly on
tiny insects,
which it obtains
by 'gleaning' –
picking them off
leaves with its
bill.

# Garden Warbler
*Sylvia borin*

One of our least known and most
unobtrusive songbirds, this widespread
summer visitor from Africa is easily
overlooked, and even when seen may be
hard to identify because of its general
lack of obvious field marks. Despite its
name, it is not a common visitor to
gardens, and is best looked for in mature
woodland with open canopies.

## Appearance
A large warbler, greyish-brown in overall
appearance, and with few obvious
identification features. Most similar to
the Blackcap in shape, but lacks the black
or brown cap, and its plumage is more
olive coloured in tone. Perhaps the best
field mark is the plain, open face and
beady eye, with only a very faint eye-
stripe. It has a thick, greyish bill and dark
legs. Like most warblers, it is best
identified by its song – though that too is
difficult as it may be very similar to that
of the Blackcap.

## Behaviour
A shy and elusive bird, often skulking in
low vegetation, though singing males may
sit in a more prominent and visible
position, especially in mid May when
they return to Europe from Africa. In
autumn it may be seen feeding on berries
before embarking on the long journey
south.

WARBLERS

Adult                    Juvenile

## Breeding
Builds a cup-shaped nest in thick foliage, usually
near to the ground, and lays 4-5 pale eggs with fine
brown spots, incubated for 10-12 days. Young fledge
after only 9-12 days (one of the quickest of any
European breeding bird). One, sometimes two,
broods.

## When & Where
A summer visitor, but one of the last to arrive,
usually in early to mid May, and leaving early too, in
late August or early September. Reasonably
widespread but very thinly and patchily distributed
throughout lowland England and Wales; less
common in southern Scotland, and only a few pairs
in Ireland. It is currently declining.

WARBLERS

| J | F | M | A | M | J |
| J | A | S | O | N | D |

## ID FACT FILE

**SIZE**
Length 13cm
(5in). About the
size of a Great Tit.

**LOOKALIKES**
May be confused
with Garden
Warbler, or
superficially with
Marsh Tit.

**VOICE**
Distinctive, fluty
song,
reminiscent of
Blackbird in tone
but at a higher
pitch. Call a hard
'tac'.

**FEEDING**
In summer feeds
mainly on
insects, but in
autumn and
winter has a
more varied diet
including berries.

# Blackcap
*Sylvia atricapilla*

One of our commonest and most
widespread summer visitors, this warbler
was once exclusively a summer visitor to
Britain. However, in the past couple of
decades birds from continental Europe
have begun to spend the whole of the
winter here, often visiting gardens to
feed on berries and fruit. Meanwhile the
British breeding population migrates less
far than other warblers, wintering in
Iberia and North Africa. The species
arrives back early in Britain, a habit
which once gave it the folk name of
'March Nightingale'.

## Appearance
If seen well, Blackcaps are fairly easy to
identify: a large, fairly bulky, grey warbler
with paler underparts, and a black cap
(male) or chestnut-brown one (female).
Beware of confusion with the Marsh Tit,
which is superficially similar in
appearance but noticeably smaller and
plumper, and has a very different outline
and habits.

## Behaviour
In spring and summer Blackcaps are best
sought out by listening for the male's
distinctive fluty song – Blackbird-like but
higher in pitch and faster in pace. In
autumn and winter this species is much
more likely to visit smaller gardens,
either feeding on berries or coming to

WARBLERS

Adult male
(summer)

Adult female
(summer)

Juvenile

feeders. Very partial to hanging 'fat bars', which provide a quick burst of much needed energy.

## Breeding
Builds its nest in low, thick bushes or shrubs, laying 4-6 pale eggs with fine brown spots, incubated for 10-12 days. Young fledge after 10-13 days. One or two broods.

## When & Where
Summer visitors arrive in March or April and depart in September or October. Winter visitors overlap, arriving in autumn and departing in the spring, and are commoner in the east of Britain. It is widespread throughout Britain apart from northern Scotland and highland areas; fairly scarce in Ireland.

| J | F | M | A | M | J |
|---|---|---|---|---|---|
| J | A | S | O | N | D |

## ID FACT FILE

**SIZE**
Length 10-11cm
(4-4.5in). One of
our smallest
songbirds.

**LOOKALIKES**
Willow Warbler,
which is longer-
winged and has
a brighter yellow-
green plumage.

**VOICE**
The famous
repeated two-
note phrase:
'chiff' and
'chaff'! Also a
distinctive 'hoo-
eeet' call,
especially in
autumn.

**FEEDING**
Feeds mainly on
small insects
gleaned from the
surface of
leaves, though
wintering birds
have recently
adapted to
taking seeds
from bird tables.

# Chiffchaff
*Phylloscopus collybita*

One of our commonest and most familiar
warblers, this tiny bird usually announces
its arrival in early spring with the familiar
song which gives the species its name: a
repeated series of two notes. In recent
years Chiffchaffs have also begun to
spend the winter in southern and western
Britain, usually in areas near water where
insects are more likely to be found.

## Appearance
Superficially very similar to the Willow
Warbler, though more olive and brown in
tone, and with a less prominent eye-
stripe and dark legs. There are subtle
differences in shape: the Chiffchaff is
more short-winged and stocky than its
cousin. It is best identified by its famous
song, which can be heard from early in
the spring season, before most other
migrants have returned.

## Behaviour
It is most easily observed when feeding
or singing, as it flits around the canopy of
trees, flicking its wings. Males often
deliver their famous song while sitting
out on a prominent perch, especially
early on in the breeding season when
they are hoping to attract a mate.

## Breeding
Hides its nest very low in dense
vegetation or on the ground, and lays 4-7

Adult
(spring)

Adult
(autumn)

Juvenile

pale eggs with dark spots, which it incubates for
13-15 days. The young fledge after 12-15 days.
One, sometimes two, broods.

## When & where

Earliest migrants return from their Mediterranean
winter quarters in March and stay until September.
During the breeding season Chiffchaffs are common
and widespread throughout England, Wales and
most of Ireland; less so in Scotland. They are likely
to be heard or seen in most wooded habitats apart
from coniferous forest. Wintering birds are found
mostly in southern and western Britain and Ireland,
where the milder climate enables them to find their
insect food. Currently on the increase.

| J | F | M | A | M | J |
|---|---|---|---|---|---|
| J | A | S | O | N | D |

**SIZE**
Length 10.5-
11.5cm (4-4.5in).
Size of Blue Tit,
but much
slimmer.

**LOOKALIKES**
Chiffchaff and
Wood Warbler;
but best told
apart by song
rather than
plumage
differences.

**VOICE**
A beautiful,
rather plaintive
song, with a
series of notes
descending the
scale.

**FEEDING**
Feeds on small
insects, taken
from leaves and
other foliage.

# Willow Warbler
*Phylloscopus trochilus*

Surprisingly perhaps, the Willow Warbler
is our commonest summer visitor, with
several million pairs making the long and
arduous journey from southern Africa to
breed each year. However, its small size
and unobtrusive manner mean that it is
rarely noticed by non-birdwatchers;
though they may hear its delightful song.
Outside Britain, the species is found
right across northern Europe and Asia.
The Willow Warbler was not separated
from its close relatives until just over two
centuries ago, when Gilbert White finally
told them apart.

**Appearance**
A small, delicate green and yellowish 'leaf
warbler', with paler underparts, pale legs
and a distinctive eye-stripe. It has a
brighter appearance, longer wings, paler
legs and more prominent eye-stripe than
the Chiffchaff, and is smaller than the
Wood Warbler, with no white on its
belly. Juveniles appear very yellow,
especially underneath; and are much
brighter than young Chiffchaffs.

**Behaviour**
Willow Warblers can be found in a wide
range of wooded habitats, including
mixed or deciduous woodland, birch
scrub and even heathland. Some visit
gardens, but are less likely to be seen
there than the Chiffchaff. Males often

WARBLERS

Adult (spring)     Adult (autumn)     Juvenile

sing from a prominent perch in the spring,
especially just after they return in mid April. In
autumn Willow Warblers migrate farther than
almost all other summer visitors, spending the
winter in southern Africa.

## Breeding
It builds its nest from grasses on the ground,
concealed in low vegetation, with a domed entrance,
where it lays 4-8 eggs, incubated for 12-14 days.
Young fledge after about two weeks. Usually one
brood, but some males have two.

## When & Where
A summer visitor, arriving in April and departing
south in September. Found throughout Britain and
Ireland. Currently decreasing, perhaps because of
problems on the migratory journey or wintering
grounds.

# Goldcrest
*Regulus regulus*

## ID FACT FILE

**SIZE**
Length 9cm
(3.5in). Tiny!

**LOOKALIKES**
The rarer
Firecrest is
similar in size
but more brightly
coloured;
Chiffchaff and
Willow Warbler
lack the coloured
crown.

**VOICE**
Thin, high-
pitched 'see-see-
see' call often
the first
indication of its
presence. Song
a distinctive,
high-pitched
phrase, with a
rapid rhythm on
three repeated
notes.

**FEEDING**
Feeds on tiny
insects and other
invertebrates,
picked up using
its thin bill.

Britain and Europe's smallest bird, the
Goldcrest is closely related to the leaf
warblers such as Willow Warbler and
Chiffchaff, which it superficially
resembles. Despite its tiny size the
Goldcrest is well able to survive very
harsh winter weather, retreating deep
into forests to feed. It also joins flocks of
feeding birds such as tits, and can be
detected by its very high pitched call –
too high for many human ears to hear!

## Appearance

Tiny, plump and compact (weighing just
five grams – the equivalent of a 20 pence
coin or sheet of paper), this little
greenish-coloured bird is best identified
by its orange (male) or yellow (female)
crown, which is often shown
prominently, especially during a
courtship display or when faced with a
predator. Closer views reveal a black,
beady eye, and pale wing bar. In flight it
appears short-winged and short-tailed:
like a small ball of feathers!

## Behaviour

Often hides deep in foliage, where it
gleans for tiny insects, hovering on
whirring wings as it does so. It can be
very confiding, especially in winter and is
often found in gardens, especially those
with conifers, which provide food and
dense foliage for the birds to breed.

WARBLERS

Adult male

Adult female

Juvenile

### Breeding

Builds a very small nest, hanging off the end of a twig, often in a conifer tree or bush, where it cannot be seen by predators. Lays 7-12 tiny eggs, pale with fine buff spots, incubated for 16 days. Young fledge after 19 days. Two broods, often close together, so that the young from the first brood are still being fed while the second are in the nest.

### When & where

Resident, though immigrants from Scandinavia augment numbers in autumn and winter. Common and widespread throughout most of Britain and Ireland, but numbers are currently decreasing.

# Firecrest
*Regulus ignicapillus*

## ID FACT FILE

**SIZE**
Length 9cm
(3.5in).

**LOOKALIKES**
Very similar to
Goldcrest,
though
marginally bulkier
and more
colourful, with a
redder crest and
distinctive head
pattern.

**VOICE**
Song series of
high-pitched
repeated notes,
lacking rhythm of
Goldcrest. Call a
high-pitched 'zit'.

**FEEDING**
Feeds on tiny
insects, obtained
by 'gleaning'
from leaves
using its small,
sharp bill.

Vying with its close relative the
Goldcrest to be Europe's smallest bird,
the Firecrest is even more attractive and
delightful than its commoner cousin. It
is more likely to be seen in mixed or
deciduous woodland than coniferous,
though like the Goldcrest it will often
nest in Norway Spruce plantations. In
autumn and winter it is often found in
mild, damper areas near coasts. It is a
rare garden visitor in Britain.

## Appearance

A tiny, bright little bird. Marginally
bigger than its commoner cousin the
Goldcrest, from which it can easily be
told apart – so long as it stays still
enough for you to notice the field marks!
Note its distinctive black eye-stripe,
fiery, reddish crown, white wing bars,
and obvious rusty-orange patch on
flanks.

## Behaviour

Like the Goldcrest, it flits around leaves
of trees to glean insects, often hovering
momentarily to do so. On breeding
grounds it is most likely to be heard
rather than seen, though in winter may
become marginally less reclusive. Also
like the Goldcrest, it may join small
flocks of tits and other woodland species
in winter, travelling together through the
wood to search for food.

WARBLERS

Adult male      Adult female      Juvenile

### Breeding

Builds a tiny nest out of moss, lichen and spiders'
webs, and lined with grass, suspended from the
end of twigs or leaves. Lays 7-12 eggs, incubated
for 14-16 days. Young fledge after about three
weeks. One, sometimes two, broods.

### When & Where

Partial migrant, found breeding throughout
continental Europe. Rare breeder in southern
Britain; also sometimes seen on migration and in
winter, especially near the southern coast. May
benefit from the onset of global warming, especially
if the incidence of mild winters increases.

FLYCATCHERS

| J | F | M | A | M | J |
|---|---|---|---|---|---|
| J | A | S | O | N | D |

## ID FACT FILE

**SIZE**
Length 14.5cm
(5.75in). About
the size of a
House Sparrow,
but slimmer.

**LOOKALIKES**
Superficially like
a warbler, but
distinctive
plumage and
shape.

**VOICE**
Series of high
pitched squeaky
notes, delivered
from a perch on
a branch.

**FEEDING**
Feeds exclusively
on small flying
insects caught
on the wing or
gleaned from
leaves.

# Spotted Flycatcher
*Muscicapa striata*

This delightful summer visitor to
Britain is now sadly decreasing in
numbers, possibly due to a lack of
insect food, or perhaps because of
drought on its African wintering
grounds. It can still be seen flycatching
for food in many rural areas, where it
tends to be found in older gardens with
stone walls, in which the birds make
their nests. It is one of our latest
summer visitors to arrive, often not
appearing until the middle of May.

### Appearance
A slim, brownish bird, with a distinctive
upright stance, beady eye and long,
thin bill which it uses to grab insects in
flight. Upperparts are a dull, palish-
brown, slightly darker on wings;
underparts buff-streaked with fine,
darker lines on the throat and sides of
breast. It is best identified by its
characteristic habit of flycatching on
long, slender wings, usually returning
to the same twig or perch on a tree or
wall.

### Behaviour
Its habit of launching itself into the air
to catch flying insects gives the species
its name. It is generally quite confiding,
with a preference for sunny, walled
gardens where it can build a nest and
catch food.

### Breeding

Builds its nest in a crevice or crack in a wall, and lays 4-6 buff or bluish eggs speckled with red, incubated for 12-14 days. Young fledge after 14 days or so. One, sometimes two broods, especially in warm, dry summers, when there is plenty of insect food available for the young birds.

Adult

Juvenile

### When & where

A summer visitor, not usually arriving until mid May, though some birds may appear from mid to late April; departing south again by August or September. Found throughout Britain and Ireland, though commonest in the south and east. It is currently undergoing a major decline, which it may be difficult to reverse.

TITS

| J | F | M | A | M | J |
|---|---|---|---|---|---|
| J | A | S | O | N | D |

## ID FACT FILE

**SIZE**
Length 14cm
(5.5in), the same
as a Great Tit –
but mostly tail!

**LOOKALIKES**
Unlike any other
British bird!

**VOICE**
Distinctive high-
pitched contact
call, repeated to
keep in touch
with other
members of its
flock.

**FEEDING**
Feeds on tiny
insects and also
spiders, obtained
by picking off
leaves and bark
with that tiny bill.

# Long-tailed Tit
*Aegithalos caudatus*

This delightful little bird is one of our most distinctive residents: its long tail and fluffy body make it hard to confuse with any other species. A sociable bird, it usually travels in family parties, in which the birds call to one another as they go in order to keep contact and warn each other of the danger from predators. Its amazing nest once gave it the country name 'bumbarrel'.

## Appearance

Given good views, this little bird is hard to mistake for any other species. Its plumage is a combination of dark brown, white, cream and pinkish-buff, though young birds are less colourful and have darker markings on the head and neck. It is shaped like a ball of fluff with a long tail – the tail itself makes up almost two-thirds of the total length of the bird!

## Behaviour

Usually heard before it is seen, uttering high-pitched contact calls with other members of its flock. When it does appear, it usually stops momentarily to feed, before passing on with the rest of the birds. It can be extremely confiding, virtually ignoring human observers, especially during the autumn and winter when finding food during short daylight hours is a priority.

TITS

Adult (Britain and Western Europe)

Adult (Northern Europe)

Juvenile

## Breeding

Builds an extraordinary, barrel-shaped
nest out of feathers, spiders' webs and
lichen, low in a bush such as a bramble. Lays
7-12 tiny white eggs, incubated for 13-17 days.
Young fledge after 15-16 days, accompanying their
parents for some time afterwards. One brood.

## When & where

Found throughout England, Wales and much of
Scotland; scarcer and less widespread in Ireland. It
often visits gardens in family parties, especially after
the breeding season and during the autumn and
winter. The Long-tailed Tit suffers very badly from
hard winter weather, but is currently increasing,
thanks to mild winters.

| J | F | M | A | M | J |
|---|---|---|---|---|---|
| J | A | S | O | N | D |

# Marsh Tit
*Parus palustris*

## ID FACT FILE

**Size**
Length 11.5cm (4.5in).

**Lookalikes**
Superficially similar to Coal Tit or Blackcap; much more likely to be confused with rarer Willow Tit.

**Voice**
Song a repeated phrase of notes rather like Blue Tit. Call an explosive 'pit-choo' – often the best indication of its presence.

**Feeding**
Feeds mainly on insects during the breeding season, and nuts and seeds in autumn and winter.

Although not as widespread as its commoner relatives, the Marsh Tit is nevertheless a fairly regular visitor to gardens, especially in rural areas of England and Wales. It is less likely to spend time on feeders than other tits, as it comes low down the 'pecking order', so it prefers to take a seed or nut and feed nearby. It is easily confused with the very similar looking Willow Tit: indeed, the two species were not officially separated from each other until just over a century ago.

**Appearance**
A medium-sized tit, mainly brown with paler underparts and a black cap and bib. It is less bulky and not so bull-necked as the Willow Tit and has a glossy (not dull matt) cap and no pale patch on its wing. It is bulkier and less colourful than the Coal Tit and lacks the pale patch on the back of its neck.

**Behaviour**
Like all tits, it is partial to feeding on seeds and peanuts, and will regularly come to bird tables and feeders, especially in gardens near woodland. Yet it is shyer and less dominant than Blue or Great Tits, often waiting its turn to feed. Usually solitary or seen in twos or threes, but the Marsh Tit may join mixed tit flocks and roam around woodland for food in winter.

TITS

**Breeding**
Builds its nest in a hole in a
tree (or occasionally a nestbox),
laying 7-11 white eggs spotted
with red, incubated for 13-15
days. Young fledge after 17-21
days. One brood.

Adult

Juvenile

**When & where**
Found in suitable broadleaved
woodland habitat and large,
rural or suburban gardens throughout England and
Wales where it is resident, with a very few breeding
in southern Scotland. Completely absent from
Ireland. Currently in decline, though the onset of
global warming may help it spread northwards.

| J | F | M | A | M | J |
|---|---|---|---|---|---|
| J | A | S | O | N | D |

## ID FACT FILE

**SIZE**
Length 11.5cm
(4.5in). Size of
Blue Tit but often
appears even
smaller.

**LOOKALIKES**
Superfcially
similar to Marsh
and Willow Tits.

**VOICE**
Rhythmic song
rather like gentle
version of Great
Tit. Calls a series
of thin, high-
pitched squeaks,
inaudible to some
human ears.

**FEEDING**
Feeds on tiny
insects during
spring and
summer, but
from autumn
onwards will visit
gardens in
search of seeds
and nuts from
feeders.

# Coal Tit
*Parus ater*

This neat little bird is usually found in or
near coniferous woods and forests, though
it is adaptable enough to venture into
gardens in search of a free meal. Like all
its family, it performs acrobatic feats in
order to obtain food, though usually
defers to its commoner relatives in the
feeding station pecking order, in which it
comes well below Great and Blue Tits and
just below the Marsh Tit. It is currently
increasing thanks to the availability of food
and conifer plantations in which to breed.

## Appearance
A small, active little bird, with a
distinctive white patch on the nape (back
of the neck), white cheeks and a black
head and bib, the combination of which
allow you to tell it apart from all other
members of its family. Its upperparts are
brown with a white wingbar and its
underparts white, tinged with buff.
Overall it appears quite colourful, despite
the main colours being black and brown.

## Behaviour
A sociable bird, often feeding with other
tit species, especially during autumn and
winter when they form mixed flocks to
search for food in woods and gardens. It
is fonder of conifers than its relatives, and
is often seen in the company of
Goldcrests, with which it shares a high-
pitched call.

TITS

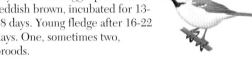

Adult

Juvenile

**Breeding**
Builds a compact nest
out of moss, often in a
cavity in a branch or tree stump.
Lays 8-9 white eggs spotted with
reddish brown, incubated for 13-
18 days. Young fledge after 16-22
days. One, sometimes two,
broods.

**When & where**
Found throughout suitable habitat in Britain and
Ireland apart from the extreme north, including the
Scottish Highlands as well as in most suburbs and
the edge of cities, especially where there are
extensive areas of wooded habitat where it can
breed. Resident.

| J | F | M | A | M | J |
| J | A | S | O | N | D |

## ID FACT FILE

**SIZE**
Length 11.5cm
(4.5in).

**LOOKALIKES**
Superficially
similar to other
tits, but the only
one with blue in
its plumage.

**VOICE**
A variety of
chattering calls
and song, with
trills and
scolding sounds,
often used as
contact calls with
other members
of a flock.

**FEEDING**
During nesting
time feeds mainly
on insects,
especially
caterpillars. In
autumn and
winter will also
take seeds and
peanuts.

# Blue Tit
*Parus caeruleus*

Our commonest and most widespread species of tit, found in virtually every garden in the country, and as a result vies with the Robin as Britain's favourite bird. It was amongst the first kinds of bird to adapt to artificial seed and peanut feeders, and has also learned to raid milk bottles in search of cream. It also readily takes to breeding in artificial nestboxes, a useful substitute for natural nest holes, which means they are usually present in gardens all year round. Indeed, during one winter, up to 1,000 different Blue Tits may visit a single garden.

## Appearance
Unmistakable, with powder-blue cap, black and white face pattern, green back and yellow belly. It is much smaller than the Great Tit, which is black on the head and shows no blue anywhere in its plumage.

## Behaviour
This cheeky and confident little bird, often barges to the front of the queue to take food, endearing it to many householders, though in reality it usually defers to the larger Great Tit in the pecking order. In winter it forms flocks with other tit species, which do a circuit of gardens to maximise their ability to find food.

### Breeding

A hole nester, building
a nest from grass lined
with moss and feathers,
and laying from 5-16
(usually 10-12) white eggs with a
few spots, incubated for 13-16
days. Young fledge after 16-22
days. One brood. It often attempts
to nest very early in the season, but
if cold weather causes this to fail, it will try again
later.

Adult

Juvenile

### When & where

Found throughout Britain and Ireland apart from
the extreme north and west, and outlying islands.
Currently on the increase, probably due to a
combination of very mild winters and plenty of
available food provided by householders. Resident.

| J | F | M | A | M | J |
|---|---|---|---|---|---|
| J | A | S | O | N | D |

## ID FACT FILE

**SIZE**
Length 14cm
(5.5in). Size of
House Sparrow.

**LOOKALIKES**
Superficially
similar to Blue
Tit but black in
plumage and
larger size
distinctive.

**VOICE**
The repetitive
and strident 'tea-
cher, tea-cher' is
its best known
sound; along with
a bewilderingly
wide variety of
other calls.

**FEEDING**
During the
breeding season
feeds mainly on
insects, especially
large caterpillars,
but outside this
time will take
seeds and
peanuts from
artificial feeders.

# Great Tit
*Parus major*

The largest European species in the tit family, the Great Tit is widespread and common in Britain, thanks partly to the efforts of householders providing extra supplies of food and nestboxes where this former woodland species can breed in safety. Like its smaller relatives, it has adapted well to living alongside humans, especially in gardens, and is thriving as a result. One population of Great Tits, in a wood in Oxfordshire, are amongst the most studied wild creatures in the world, having been closely observed by scientists for half a century.

## Appearance
Arguably the smartest and most brightly coloured of its family, with black head and throat, white cheeks, green back and bright lemon-yellow underparts bisected by a black bar (which is noticeably broader in the male than in the female, allowing the careful observer to tell them apart).

## Behaviour
A loud, noticeable, far from shy species, it is always amongst the first to feed if you provide a feeding station, and top of the 'pecking order' in the tit family. In spring and early summer males sing their repetitive two-note song from prominent perches, and at other times of the year can often be heard before they are seen.

TITS

Adult

Juvenile

**Breeding**
Builds a nest in a
hole in a tree or,
more often in
gardens, a nestbox.
Lays 5-11 white eggs with
reddish spots, incubated for
11-15 days. Young fledge after
three weeks, and are fed on
caterpillars. One, sometimes two,
broods.

**When & where**
Found throughout Britain and Ireland apart from
the extreme north and west, and a few outlying
islands off the coast. Very common in gardens,
including those in the centre of towns and cities.
Currently on the increase, thanks in part to mild
winters. Resident.

| J | F | M | A | M | J |
|---|---|---|---|---|---|
| J | A | S | O | N | D |

## ID FACT FILE

**SIZE**
Length 14cm
(5.5in). Size of
Great Tit, but
appears larger
and bulkier.

**LOOKALIKES**
Seen well, like
no other British
bird!

**VOICE**
Loud, echoing
'pee-uu' call,
often the best
way to detect the
bird's presence,
especially in
spring.

**FEEDING**
Feeds mainly on
insects in the
breeding season,
and seeds and
nuts in autumn
and winter. Will
regularly visit
bird tables and
seed and nut
feeders.

# Nuthatch
*Sitta europaea*

This common but often overlooked
woodland bird has a unique feature: it is
the only British species of bird able to
climb down the trunks and branches of
trees as well as up. In recent years it has
adapted well to artificial feeders, and is
now a regular visitor to many larger
gardens, especially those near natural
woods and forests. Often detected by its
variety of loud, penetrating calls coming
from somewhere in the foliage, the
Nuthatch is then seen as it crawls along,
up or down a branch or tree trunk.

## Appearance
Seen well, the Nuthatch is unmistakable
simply by its actions. It has attractive
plumage, with steel-blue upperparts,
orange underparts and a black 'bandit
mask' giving it a rather fierce appearance.
It often resembles a small woodpecker in
its movement and habits, though no
British woodpeckers have the same
colour combination.

## Behaviour
Usually first seen clambering around the
trunk or large branches of a tree,
sometimes tapping the wood with its
powerful bill in the manner of a
woodpecker. In spring, males sing from a
prominent perch on the end of a branch,
and are generally much easier to see. In
winter it may join species such as tits and

NUTHATCH AND TREECREEPERS

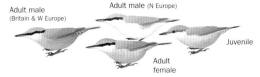

Adult male
(Britain & W Europe)

Adult male (N Europe)

Adult
female

Juvenile

Treecreepers in mixed flocks, searching for food.
Look out for its acrobatic ability to climb vertically
downwards.

**Breeding**
Nests in holes in trees, laying 6-8 white eggs spotted
with red, incubated for 13-18 days. Young fledge
after 23-24 days. One brood.

**When & where**
Resident, and fairly sedentary, rarely travelling very
far from its home territory. Common in mixed and
deciduous woodland throughout England and Wales
apart from parts of eastern England. A few breed in
southern Scotland, but it is absent from Ireland.
Currently increasing and extending its range
northwards, probably due to global warming.

# Treecreeper
*Certhia familiaris*

## ID FACT FILE

**SIZE**
Length 12.5cm (5in). Smaller and slimmer than Nuthatch.

**LOOKALIKES**
Seen well, like no other British species – though very similar to Europe's Short-toed Treecreeper.

**VOICE**
A thin, very high pitched trill, easily overlooked. Call a high pitched 'tsee'.

**FEEDING**
Feeds entirely on small insects and grubs taken from ther surface of or beneath the bark of trees.

There can hardly be any other British bird which has such an appropriate name: this woodland species is invariably glimpsed as it crawls, mouse-like, around trunks and branches of trees, in search of its insect prey. It is very badly affected by hard winters, especially when glazed frosts cover the twigs and branches of trees, which means that it can no longer find food.

## Appearance
With its unique tree climbing habits it cannot really be confused with any other bird, though superficially may look like a tit or Goldcrest. It is much smaller and slimmer than the Nuthatch or any woodpeckers, with brown upperparts, whitish underparts shading to brown on flanks, and a long, decurved bill. Its combination of colours and markings, and its habit of creeping around, may make it quite hard to detect. Unlike the Nuthatch, it is not able to climb down tree trunks.

## Behaviour

As its name suggests, this species spends most of its life creeping up and along tree trunks and branches, probing for tiny morsels of food with its delicate, thin bill. It is generally very sedentary, rarely flying anything but a very short distance from tree to tree.

NUTHATCH AND TREECREEPERS

## Breeding

Nests inside a crack or crevice in a tree, laying 5-6 white eggs with a few brownish spots, incubated for 13-15 days. Young fledge after 14-16 days. One, but also often two, broods. It will occasionally breed in special wedge-shaped artificial nestbox if placed in suitable habitat.

## When & where

Resident and highly sedentary, the Treecreeper is found in most British and Irish woods, though is absent from the extreme north and west of Britain. It occasionally visits gardens, though usually only those in fairly rural areas with large trees in or nearby. Currently increasing thanks to the recent run of very mild winters.

Adult

Juvenile

| J | F | M | A | M | J |
|---|---|---|---|---|---|
| J | A | S | O | N | D |

# Short-toed Treecreeper
*Certhia brachydactyla*

## ID FACT FILE

**Size**
Length 12.5cm
(5in). Smaller
and slimmer
than Nuthatch.

**Lookalikes**
Treecreeper –
can only really be
distinguished
when trapped
and examined
feather by feather
in the hand.

**Voice**
Similar to that
of Treecreeper,
but slightly
louder and more
forceful.

**Feeding**
Tiny invertebrates
and their grubs,
obtained with its
sharp, decurved
bill.

This southern and western counterpart of
the Treecreeper is almost impossible to
identify with certainty in the field, and as
a result may have been overlooked in
Britain, where there are only a handful of
records, mostly at bird observatories on
the south coast. In parts of western
Europe, including most of France, Spain
and Portugal, it has replaced the
Treecreeper and is the only member of
its family present.

## Appearance
Very similar to the Treecreeper, it has
brownish upperparts with darker streaks,
pale underparts, and the same long,
decurved bill – so it can only be told
apart with certainty in the hand. In fact
this species has a very slightly longer bill
and browner streaking on the flanks than
its relative, but is best identified by its
geographical location, or with a lot of
practice, by its song.

## Behaviour
Like the Treecreeper, it spends most of
its life crawling around the trunks and
branches of trees in search of tiny insects,
which it prises out from beneath the bark
or from crevices with its sharp, pointed
bill. Also like its relative, it rarely flies
more than the distance from one tree to
another; though a few have, amazingly,
crossed the Channel!

## Breeding
Nests inside a crack or crevice in the side of a tree, or sometimes in an old woodpecker's hole, like the Treecreeper. Lays 4-7 white eggs with very faint reddish or purple markings at the broader end, incubated for 13-15 days. Young fledge after 15-18 days. Usually two broods.

## When & Where
Resident in suitable wooded habitat throughout southern and western Europe, including Spain, France, Italy, Germany and the Low Countries. Very rare vagrant to southern Britain. Its range overlaps with Treecreeper in parts of France, Germany and central Europe.

Adult

Juvenile

ORIOLES

## ID FACT FILE

**SIZE**
Length 24cm
(9.5in). About
the size of a
Blackbird.

**LOOKALIKES**
Male
unmistakable;
female may be
mistaken for
young Green
Woodpecker or if
seen poorly, a
thrush.

**VOICE**
A lyrical and fluty
series of four
notes: 'wee-la-
wee-ooo' – once
heard, never
forgotten.

**FEEDING**
Feeds on
insects,
especially
caterpillars,
taken from
foliage of trees
or the ground.

# Golden Oriole
*Oriolus oriolus*

This stunning but shy bird rarely reveals its presence, apart from its distinctive and fluty song. Once only a rare spring or occasionally autumn visitor to Britain, in recent decades it has colonised parts of southern and eastern England as a breeding bird, though its elusive nature means that it is still very hard to find. On the continent it is more common and widespread, occasionally nesting in parks and wooded gardens.

## Appearance
The male oriole is quite simply unmistakable, with his bright golden-yellow plumage, dagger-shaped red bill and black on the wings. The female of the species is much less bright in colour, being dull, greenish-yellow overall with pale greyish underparts. In flight the Oriole appears about Blackbird sized, though with longer wings and tail: females may resemble juvenile Green Woodpeckers (though are much smaller in size), while males look like flying lemons! The flight action itself is undulating, rather like that of a woodpecker or thrush.

## Behaviour
Generally skulks high in the thick foliage of trees such as poplars, rarely revealing its presence apart from when it flies and shows its gaudy plumage.

ORIOLES

Adult male · Adult female · Juvenile

It is often solitary or during the breeding season found in pairs.

## Breeding
Breeds high in tall trees, building its nest from grass in a tree fork, usually a considerable height above the ground. It lays 3-4 eggs, which both male and female incubate for about 16-17 days. They fledge after another 16-17 days.

## When & Where
A summer visitor to much of continental Europe south of Scandinavia, though rarely seen well. Breeds in small numbers in eastern Britain, usually in conifer plantations. It winters in sub-Saharan Africa and on migration may also be seen at coastal sites, especially on the east coast and in the Scilly Isles.

CROWS

| J | F | M | A | M | J |
| J | A | S | O | N | D |

## ID FACT FILE

**Size**
Length 34-35cm
(13.5-14in). Size
of Feral Pigeon.

**Lookalikes**
Seen well, more
or less
unmistakable.

**Voice**
A harsh screech;
also a mewing
call rather like
that of the
Buzzard.

**Feeding**
Like other
members of the
crow family, Jays
will eat a wide
variety of food
including acorns,
insects and
birds' eggs and
chicks.

# Jay
*Garrulus glandarius*

Perhaps because of its bright plumage
and secretive behaviour, the Jay does not
share the Magpie's status as public
enemy number one – even though like its
cousin it also takes the eggs and chicks of
breeding songbirds to supplement its
diet. A shy bird, the Jay is often
overlooked during the spring and
summer; it becomes much more obvious
in autumn when there are often large
invasions of birds from continental
Europe to the British Isles. Like all
members of the crow family, it is
intelligent, inquisitive and highly
adaptable.

## Appearance

Seen well, it cannot really be mistaken
for any other species. A large (pigeon-
sized) bird, with mainly pinkish-brown
plumage, which can appear different
shades depending on the prevailing light.
It also has a black and white speckled
crest and a distinctive blue patch on the
wing; in flight it shows a prominent white
rump, especially obvious when the bird
flies away from you!

## Behaviour

For its size, it is quite a shy and secretive
bird, especially during the breeding
season. It is often seen in flight, when its
shape and bounding flight action are
distinctive even at some distance. It will

CROWS

Adult

Juvenile

Adult

sometimes visit bird tables in search of
nuts, and also feed on lawns. When angry
it raises its crest to scare off rivals.

## Breeding
Builds a cup-shaped nest from twigs, often placed in
a tree fork. Lays 5-8 pale, olive-coloured eggs
shaded with brown speckles, incubated for 16-17
days. Young fledge after 19-23 days. One brood.

## When & where
Resident, although continental immigrants boost
numbers in autumn and winter; with some years
seeing a full scale invasion from Europe. Found
throughout England, Wales and southern Scotland,
the Jay is also thinly spread in Ireland, where it is
considered to be a separate race from its British
counterpart. Currently increasing, thanks to its
adaptable habits.

CROWS

| J | F | M | A | M | J |
|---|---|---|---|---|---|
| J | A | S | O | N | D |

## ID FACT FILE

**SIZE**
Length 44-46cm
(17-18in). Size of
Carrion Crow, but
much slimmer
with longer tail.

**LOOKALIKES**
None.

**VOICE**
A loud, harsh
and familiar
rattle, like a child
imitating a
machine gun!

**FEEDING**
Despite its
reputation, feeds
mainly on
insects, nuts and
any other scraps
it can find, often
scavenging road
kills. During the
breeding season
will also raid
nests to take
chicks and eggs.

# Magpie
*Pica pica*

The bird which people either love or
hate, the Magpie has become something
of a pantomime villain in the past few
years, as it has been unfairly blamed for
the decline of songbirds. Others regard it
as a handsome and intelligent bird. In
medieval folklore its black and white
plumage and inquisitive habits led it to
be condemned as an evil bird, associated
with witches. After suffering major
declines at the hands of gamekeepers,
who blamed it for taking eggs and chicks
of gamebirds, the Magpie is now
undergoing a population boom,
especially in leafy towns and suburbs.

### Appearance
An unmistakable bird, apparently black
and white until a closer view reveals
subtle shades of blue and green on the
wings and tail. Its wings are rounded,
enabling it to fly through dense foliage,
and the tail is long and graduated for the
same reason. In flight it appears slender
and long-tailed.

### Behaviour
A noisy, sociable member of the crow
family, easily seen and heard, making it
appear that there are more magpies than
there actually are. Birds often squabble
amongst themselves. It is often seen in
flocks of anything between a handful of
birds and several dozen; giving rise to
famous rhymes associated with luck.

CROWS

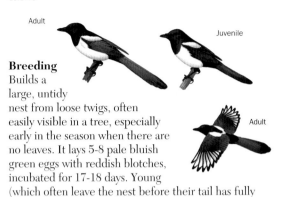

Adult

Juvenile

Adult

## Breeding
Builds a large, untidy nest from loose twigs, often easily visible in a tree, especially early in the season when there are no leaves. It lays 5-8 pale bluish green eggs with reddish blotches, incubated for 17-18 days. Young (which often leave the nest before their tail has fully grown) fledge after 22-28 days. One brood.

## When & where
Resident throughout England, Wales and Ireland, and in parts of eastern and southern Scotland, though generally absent from the highlands and islands. Currently increasing, probably because it is so well adapted to living alongside human beings.

| J | F | M | A | M | J |
|---|---|---|---|---|---|
| J | A | S | O | N | D |

## ID FACT FILE

**SIZE**
Length 33-34cm
(13-13.5in). Size
of small pigeon.

**LOOKALIKES**
Superficially like
Carrion Crow and
Rook, but much
smaller and
different shape.

**VOICE**
A distinctive
'chak', often
followed by a
gentler second
note, usually
uttered in flight.

**FEEDING**
Feeds on a wide
variety of plant
and animal
items, and will
readily come to
bird tables and
feeding stations.

# Jackdaw
*Corvus monedula*

The Jackdaw has always been a firm
favourite for its cheeky appearance and
sociable behaviour. Like the other
members of its family, it is highly
intelligent and adaptable, and has
learned quickly to take advantage of
human beings. Known for collecting
objects, especially bright shiny ones, and
can also be tamed.

## Appearance

The Jackdaw is much smaller than its
relatives the Rook and Carrion Crow,
with blackish upperparts, greyish
underparts, and a distinctive pale grey
patch around the back of the head and
neck. It also has a distinctive, large-
headed shape, a shorter bill than other
members of its family, and a dark, beady
eye. In flight it appears smaller and
shorter winged than other crows, and is
usually identified by its distinctive
'chacking' call.

## Behaviour

A sociable bird, Jackdaws often gather in
large flocks (sometimes alongside other
crow species such as Rooks and Carrion
Crows) to feed, especially in seed fields
or open grassy areas where food is
available. They may also be seen in large,
noisy flocks flying overhead to roost just
before dusk, especially during the
autumn and winter. The Jackdaw often

CROWS

Adult

Juvenile

Adult

visits gardens, especially those in villages
or near parks, in order to grab food.

## Breeding

Normally nests in a hole in a tree or a crevice in a
stone wall, building a loose nest from sticks, and
laying 4-6 pale bluish-green eggs, with dark
blotches, which are incubated for 17-18 days. Young
fledge after 4-5 weeks, and often accompany their
parents in family groups afterwards. One brood.

## When & Where

Common throughout rural and suburban areas of
England, Wales, and southern and eastern Scotland,
and very common in Ireland. Currently increasing,
thanks to its ability to live alongside human beings.

CROWS

| J | F | M | A | M | J |
| J | A | S | O | N | D |

## ID FACT FILE

**SIZE**
Length 45-47cm
(18-18.5in).
Slightly larger
than Rook;
smaller than
Raven.

**LOOKALIKES**
Rook and Raven.

**VOICE**
A harsh cawing
sound, often
uttered in flight.

**FEEDING**
Feeds on almost
anything! For
example: seeds,
insects, road
kills, eggs, baby
birds, bread, and
unmentionable
items scavenged
from waste sites.
Thrives on our
wasteful society.

# Carrion Crow
*Corvus corone*

The classic black crow, often regarded as almost as much of a villain as its black and white cousin the Magpie, for its habit of feeding on eggs and baby birds; and also perhaps because it has a sinister appearance. Yet like other members of its family, the Carrion Crow is one of the most intelligent and interesting of all birds. Lively and adaptable, it is destined to thrive this century.

## Appearance
The Carrion Crow is the only completely black bird commonly seen in Britain – the noticeably larger Raven is generally confined to upland areas. It is distinguished from the Rook by its all black face and bill, and bulkier appearance; and from the Jackdaw by its much larger size and different shape and colour. In flight its long, broad wings and thick set body give it a fearsome appearance.

## Behaviour
Noisy, sociable and liable to bully smaller birds out of the way, especially when food is at stake. It often visits gardens, especially where food is put out on the lawn or a bird table. Crows sometimes gather together in huge flocks, especially at some winter roosts, when they can present an awesome sight and sound as they fly overhead, calling as they go.

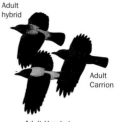

Adult
hybrid

Adult
Carrion

Adult Hooded

## Breeding
Builds a large, untidy nest from twigs, often high in the branches of a tree, and easily visible (crows have few enemies). Lays 4-6 pale, bluish-green eggs, with reddish-brown blotches, incubated for 17-21 days. Young fledge after 4-5 weeks, but usually hang around with their parents afterwards. One brood.

## When & where
Resident and widely distributed throughout urban and rural habitats in England, Wales and southern and eastern Scotland. In north and west Scotland and most of Ireland it is replaced by the Hooded Crow, now regarded as a full species. Numbers are currently increasing.

CROWS

| J | F | M | A | M | J |
|---|---|---|---|---|---|
| J | A | S | O | N | D |

### ID FACT FILE

**SIZE**
Length 45-47cm (18-18.5in), the size of a Carrion Crow.

**LOOKALIKES**
Superfcially similar to other large crows, but grey in plumage distinctive. Jackdaw also has grey, but only on back of neck.

**VOICE**
Loud, raucous cawing sound, very similar to that of Carrion Crow, and usually uttered in flight.

**FEEDING**
Omnivorous, taking all kinds of food where available, including invertebrates and grain.

# Hooded Crow
*Corvus cornix*

Until very recently this distinctive member of the crow family was presumed to be a race of the Carrion Crow. However, in the past decade scientists have finally 'split' the two, and it now has full species status. The Hooded Crow has a very unusual and fragmented distribution across Europe, being found in north and west Britain and Ireland, and also eastern Europe, with the Carrion Crow dominant in between. There is a 'hybrid zone' between the two species in Scotland.

### Appearance

The only large crow with substantial areas of grey on its plumage: its black head and wings contrast with its grey body, giving a piebald effect especially noticeable in flight, where the 'hooded' appearance is evident. It often appears to be slimmer than Carrion Crow, but this may be an optical illusion caused by the paler plumage.

### Behaviour

Like all members of the crow family, Hooded Crows (or 'Hoodies' as they are affectionately known in Scotland) are highly adaptable and opportunistic, often hanging around human habitation to see what it can get! It is generally found on farmland, often in large flocks with other members of the crow family such as Rooks, Jackdaws and occasionally Ravens.

CROWS

Juvenile Carrion

Juvenile Hooded

Adult Carrion

Adult Hooded

## Breeding

Breeds in a tree or occasionally on a cliff or rock, building a loose, untidy nest out of sticks, lined with plant material such as leaves and grass. Lays 3-7 eggs, incubated for 18-20 days. Young leave the nest after about 4-5 weeks, but hang around with their parents for another couple of weeks.

## When & Where

Mainly found in eastern and northern Europe, including the far north and west of Scotland and the whole of Ireland. A rare visitor to southern Scotland, England and Wales (especially the island of Anglesey), usually appearing in ones or twos in the winter months. Resident.

STARLINGS

| J | F | M | A | M | J |
| J | A | S | O | N | D |

## ID FACT FILE

**SIZE**
Length 21.5cm (8.5in). Smaller than thrush or Blackbird.

**LOOKALIKES**
None.

**VOICE**
Starlings are great mimics, able to imitate many other birds as well as artificial sounds such as mobile phones and car alarms!

**FEEDING**
Fairly catholic in taste, and able to feed on seeds and nuts provided by ourselves. Natural food includes invertebrates on lawns and grassy fields, obtained by probing with its sharp bill.

# Starling
*Sturnus vulgaris*

One of the most familiar yet often overlooked town and garden birds, the Starling is also one of the most attractive, with complex social behaviour – and when seen close up, a stunningly iridescent plumage. In the winter months Starlings gather in huge flocks to roost, in order to keep warm and avoid danger from predators. However, a major decline in recent years means that many former roosts are but a shadow of their former size.

## Appearance

At first sight a dull brownish-black bird; but take a closer look and you will see a greenish sheen to the dark plumage. During the breeding season both sexes develop tiny pale spots and streaks, and males in particular can appear very handsome indeed. Juvenile Starlings often puzzle observers, as they are brown and nondescript; but they have a similar size, shape and habits to the adults, so should be fairly easy to identify.

## Behaviour

Starlings are sociable, almost always seen in large, noisy flocks, squabbling amongst each other for food. Very familiar in gardens, adapting readily to obtaining food from all kinds of different sources. Roosting flocks can be seen at several famous sites, including Brighton Pier in

Adult male (summer)    Adult male (winter)    Two immature stages    Juvenile

East Sussex, where in winter they put on a daily show for the tourists!

## Breeding
Usually nests in a hole or crack in a tree, wall or building, laying 4-7 pale blue eggs, incubated for 12-15 days. Young fledge after three weeks. One or two broods. Young usually hang around in flocks with their parents for some time after fledging.

## When & where
Resident, with continental immigrants in autumn and winter. Common throughout Britain and Ireland apart from the extreme highlands. Birds in Shetland and the Western Isles are brighter, and of a different race from their mainland counterparts. Currently decreasing for largely unknown reasons.

SPARROWS

| J | F | M | A | M | J |
|---|---|---|---|---|---|
| J | A | S | O | N | D |

# House Sparrow
*Passer domesticus*

## ID FACT FILE

**SIZE**
Length 14-15cm
(5.5-6in), the size
of a Great Tit.

**LOOKALIKES**
Females
superficially
resemble
Dunnock and
female Chaffinch;
males similar to
Tree Sparrow.

**VOICE**
A characteristic
chirping – a
familiar sound of
built-up areas.

**FEEDING**
A variety of
seeds and
grains, and will
also take nuts
from feeders and
other kitchen
scraps. In
breeding season
feeds young on
insects.

Our most familiar bird is sadly nothing
like as common as it once was, and has
disappeared completely from some
urban areas – notably from the centre
of London, where it used to be the
commonest bird (hence the term
'Cockney Sparrer'). Nevertheless it is
still a common enough sight in much
of urban, suburban and rural Britain,
especially where traditional farming
methods mean there is still grain on
which to feed. The decline has been
blamed on several factors, including a
component in unleaded petrol which
may kill off the insects on which
sparrows feed their young.

### Appearance
With their neat black bib, grey and
brown cap and cheeky demeanour,
male House Sparrows are hard to
mistake for anything else. Females and
young birds are much more
nondescript in appearance, with pale,
buff underparts, streaked, brown
upperparts and a clear, pale stripe
behind the eye.

### Behaviour
Usually seen around human habitation,
and a common visitor to most gardens,
where its chirping sound is a familiar
one throughout the year. It is sociable
and gregarious, often gathering in small

SPARROWS

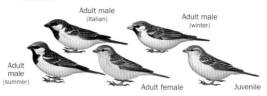

Adult male
(Italian)

Adult male
(winter)

Adult
male
(summer)

Adult female

Juvenile

flocks to feed and socialise. Used to living alongside humans, it is a regular visitor to garden feeders.

**Breeding**

Builds its nest close to human dwellings or other buildings, often under the eaves, so prefers traditional houses. Lays 3-6 pale eggs with brown and grey speckles, incubated for 11-14 days. Young fledge after 14-19 days and there may be three or even four broods in a single season. It often nests in small colonies of up to a dozen or more pairs.

**When & where**

Despite its unexplained decline, it is still a common resident throughout most of Britain and Ireland apart from the highlands and offshore islands. However, if the decline continues than large areas of Britain may find themselves without one of their most familiar birds.

FINCHES

| J | F | M | A | M | J |
|---|---|---|---|---|---|
| J | A | S | O | N | D |

# Chaffinch

*Fringilla coelebs*

## ID FACT FILE

**SIZE**
Length 14.5cm
(5.75in). About
size of House
Sparrow.

**LOOKALIKES**
Female
superficially like
House Sparrow;
both sexes can
be mistaken for
Brambling.

**VOICE**
A distinctive
song, described
as sounding like
a fast bowler
running up to
make a delivery!
Variety of calls
including 'pink'.

**FEEDING**
Seeds, grains
and in gardens on
peanuts. During
the breeding
season prefers
insect food.

One of our commonest breeding birds,
the Chaffinch is found throughout rural
Britain, and especially in well-wooded
areas, it outnumbers all other species. In
recent years it has also adapted well to
human presence, and has learned to take
advantage of food and nest sites provided
by keen gardeners. Males are one of the
handsomest of all our common birds.

## Appearance

With his bright, orange-pink underparts,
grey head and white wingbars, the male
Chaffinch is unlikely to be confused with
any other species (apart perhaps from the
much brighter pink Bullfinch, which has
a black head). Females look like a dull,
monochrome version of the male, buff-
coloured below. In flight both sexes show
a greenish rump and white wingbars, a
good identification feature.

## Behaviour

A sociable bird, though in the breeding
season males defend their territory by
singing their rather monotonous song
throughout the day. Frequent visitor to
gardens, either feeding on the lawn or
taking seed and nuts from feeders. Often
first detected by its variety of familiar and
distinctive calls. In winter Chaffinches
form large flocks, often with other seed-
eating species such as finches, sparrows
and buntings.

FINCHES

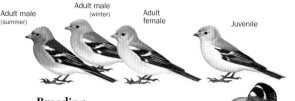

Adult male
(summer)

Adult male
(winter)

Adult
female

Juvenile

Adult
female
(summer)

**Breeding**

Builds a neat, cup-shaped nest out of
grasses, usually in the fork of a tree,
laying 3-5 pale blue eggs with darker
spots, incubated for 11-13 days. Young
fledge after 12-15 days. One or two broods.

**When & where**

Resident, though in autumn and winter visitors from
continental Europe add to the resident population.
Common and widespread in almost all parts of
Britain and Ireland, apart from the extremes of the
highlands and islands. Numbers are currently
increasing, especially in suburban areas where there
are plenty of food and nest sites available.

FINCHES

# Brambling
*Fringilla montifringilla*

## ID FACT FILE

**SIZE**
Length 14cm (5.5in). Size of Great Tit or House Sparrow.

**LOOKALIKES**
Chaffinch; but has distinctive field marks.

**VOICE**
Two calls: a gentle 'chuck-chuck', and a harsher, squeaky 'wee-eek'.

**FEEDING**
Feeds almost exclusively on seeds during the autumn and winter months, and will take advantage of feeding stations in gardens, often hopping about beneath the feeder to pick up spilt seed.

The northern European equivalent of the more familiar Chaffinch, the Brambling is one of the commonest breeding species in Europe, though only a few stay on after the winter ends to breed in Britain. In this country Bramblings mainly visit in autumn and winter, and are best looked for in beech woods, where they search for their favourite food of beech mast. Some years see much larger numbers than others, depending on the availability of food back home.

## Appearance
At first sight, the male Brambling looks like an even brighter version of the Chaffinch, but its black head, orange underparts and white rump are always distinctive. The female is also brightly coloured, but streakier and with less black on her head than the male. Juvenile birds are paler and greyer on the head and less bright below. In flight the white rump is a very useful field mark; the only other member of its family to share this feature is the Bullfinch.

## Behaviour
A sociable bird, usually seen in large flocks during the winter. Often associates with other seed eaters such as finches and buntings, feeding on stubble fields in areas where traditional farming is still practised. It will sometimes visit

FINCHES

Adult male (summer)  Adult male (winter)  Adult female (summer)  Juvenile

Female (summer)

gardens, especially in rural areas near
large areas of broadleaved or mixed
woodland, feeding on the ground beneath
bird tables, where it picks up spilt seed.

## Breeding
Only a few pairs nest in Britain each year; the
rest head north and east to Scandinavia. It lays
6-7 eggs, incubated for 11-12 days. Young fledge
after 13-14 days.

## When & where
An autumn and winter visitor, arriving in
September and October and departing in March
and April. Found in many parts of Britain, though
thinly distributed so may be hard to find and is
scarce in Ireland. More likely to visit gardens
during harsh winter weather.

FINCHES

| J | F | M | A | M | J |
|---|---|---|---|---|---|
| J | A | S | O | N | D |

## ID FACT FILE

**SIZE**
Length 11.5cm
(4.5in). Europe's
smallest finch;
size of Blue Tit.

**LOOKALIKES**
Similar to Siskin,
but smaller and
male much more
yellow, with
different bill
shape.

**VOICE**
A distinctive
jangling song,
quite like that of
the Corn Bunting.

**FEEDING**
Feeds mainly on
seeds, but in
breeding season
also takes small
insects including
caterpillars.

# Serin
*Serinus serinus*

This tiny finch is a common bird of woods, hedgerows, parks and gardens all over continental Europe, including France right up to the Channel coast. Every year overshooting spring migrants arrive on the south coast of England, and it has bred in southern counties such as Devon and Dorset several times. However, despite these attempts, it has yet to establish a foothold as a British breeding bird. Climate change may alter all that, however, enabling the species to extend its range northward, and finally become a regular British breeding bird.

## Appearance

A tiny finch, closely related to the Canary; with a round head, short forked tail and streaky plumage. Males are greenish-yellow, and in the breeding season have a bright canary-yellow head, contrasting with streaked green and yellow on the rest of the body and wings. Females are much duller in appearance, though the greenish tinge and stubby bill are usually evident.

## Behaviour

In spring and early summer, males usually sing from a prominent song post such a bush or telegraph wire. On the mainland of Europe the Serin is

FINCHES

often found in gardens and villages. Some populations migrate; others stay put for the winter.

Female (summer)

Juvenile

### Breeding
Breeds in dense foliage, where it builds a tiny nest out of grass and moss, lined with feathers or hair, and lays 3-5 eggs, incubated for 12-14 days. The young fledge after 14-16 days, but stay with the parents to be fed for at least a week afterwards. Two broods, the second sometimes started while the first young are still being fed.

### When & Where
Partial migrant, found throughout Continental Europe. Annual visitor to southern England, usually in spring. Has bred in Devon and Dorset, and may well do so again.

FINCHES

| J | F | M | A | M | J |
|---|---|---|---|---|---|
| J | A | S | O | N | D |

## ID FACT FILE

**SIZE**
Length 15cm (6in). Slightly larger than House Sparrow.

**LOOKALIKES**
Superficially similar to other green finches, but larger and less streaky. Young can look like female House Sparrow.

**VOICE**
A variety of wheezing and twittering calls. Song a combination of trills, whistles and twitters rather like that of a Canary.

**FEEDING**
During the breeding season Greenfinches mainly feed on seeds and insects, while in winter they also take peanuts.

# Greenfinch
*Carduelis chloris*

One of the commonest and most widespread members of the finch family, the Greenfinch is also a very common visitor to gardens, often staying on to breed there, and especially common in late summer when the young leave the nest. In recent years it has adapted well to living alongside humans, being a regular visitor to seed and peanut feeders, and both roosting and nesting in large hedgerows where the foliage makes a safe hiding place.

## Appearance

A large, plain (rather than streaky) finch. The adult male is a bright yellow-green, with a pale grey tinge on the wings and darker grey on the wingtips and tail. The female is slightly less bright, but usually shows some green and yellow in the plumage. Both have pale ivory-coloured bills. In flight the yellow on the wings becomes obvious. Juveniles can look almost sparrow-like, as they lack most of the green and yellow pigments in their plumage.

## Behaviour

During the breeding season males are often seen singing in a display flight, or from a high perch in a tree, in an effort to attract passing females. In late summer, autumn and winter Greenfinches form flocks, often visiting bird feeding stations,

FINCHES

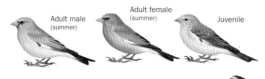

Adult male
(summer)

Adult female
(summer)

Juvenile

where they have a particular
preference for sunflower seeds.

Adult
female
(summer)

## Breeding
It often nests in colonies of several pairs,
building a cup shaped nest deep in the foliage of a
tree or dense bush, such as a cypress. Lays 3-6 pale
eggs with darker spots, incubated for 12-14 days.
Young fledge after 13-17 days. Two broods.

## When & where
Common and widespread throughout Britain apart
from northern and western Scotland; less
widespread in Ireland. Often found in gardens,
especially those near farmland or woodland, or in
suburbs with large mature trees or thick hedges.
Currently on the increase.

FINCHES

| J | F | M | A | M | J |
| J | A | S | O | N | D |

## ID FACT FILE

**SIZE**
Length 12cm
(4.75in). Slightly
larger than Blue
Tit.

**LOOKALIKES**
Seen well,
unmistakable,
though young
can cause
confusion until
they fly.

**VOICE**
Musical
twittering songs
and calls, with
trills, creating a
delightful sound.

**FEEDING**
Feeds mainly on
tiny seeds,
removed from
plants using its
specially pointed
and conical bill.
In recent years
has taken to
feeding on
sunflower seeds
from artificial
feeders, so look
out for them in
your garden!

# Goldfinch
*Carduelis carduelis*

The Goldfinch is one of our most
attractive and charming finches – an
appropriate adjective since a flock of
Goldfinches used to be known as a
'charm'! It was once popular with the
cage-bird trade, and captured by the
thousand by professional Victorian bird
collectors: fortunately it is now protected
and is thriving. Like other finches it has
learned to feed from artificial feeders,
with a marked preference for small
sunflower seeds.

## Appearance
The adults are unmistakable (both sexes
are alike), with buff underparts and back;
black on the head, wings and tail, white
on the neck and throat, and a bright
crimson face patch. They also have
golden-yellow stripes on the wings which
flash brightly when the birds take to the
air, and which give the species its
common name. Juveniles appear mainly
brownish-buff until they fly, when they
also reveal the bright-yellow stripes
across the wing.

## Behaviour
A sociable little bird, which is usually
seen in pairs or flocks of up to several
dozen birds, often chattering tunefully to
each other as they look for food, or warn
against predators or other danger. To
feed, Goldfinches perch on the tops of

FINCHES

 Adult  Juvenile

thistles, teasels and other spiky
plants to remove the seeds. When
on seed feeders they delicately
remove the seed kernel from the
shell with that sharp beak.

Adult

## Breeding
Builds a small, cup-shaped nest in the outer branches
or twigs of a tree or bush. Lays 4-6 pale eggs with
dark spots and streaks, incubated for 12-14 days.
Young fledge after 12-15 days. Two or three broods.

## When & where
Common and fairly widespread throughout
England, Wales and parts of southern and eastern
Scotland, and also found in parts of Ireland.
Resident throughout the year and numbers are
currently increasing.

FINCHES

| J | F | M | A | M | J |
|---|---|---|---|---|---|
| J | A | S | O | N | D |

## ID FACT FILE

**SIZE**
Length 12cm
(4.75in). Size of
Blue Tit; much
smaller than
Greenfinch.

**LOOKALIKES**
Similar to Serin,
but larger and
less yellow. Also
can be confused
with Greenfinch.

**VOICE**
Song a rapid
series of
twitters, trills and
wheezy notes,
rather like that of
Greenfinch. Also
a number of
wheezy calls.

**FEEDING**
Mainly feeds on
seeds and
insects, but also
takes peanuts
and sunflower
seeds.

# Siskin
*Carduelis spinus*

This tiny little finch was once a specialist of coniferous woodlands, but during the late 20th century it rapidly adapted to life in our gardens, where today it is a common and frequent visitor. It often appears in the company of its cousin the Redpoll, in mixed flocks. Siskins have a particular preference for habitats near water, especially where alder trees are found, as they enjoy feeding on their cones. Look out for them in late winter and early spring when natural food is scarce and they are most likely to visit gardens in small flocks.

## Appearance
At first sight, the Siskin looks like a smaller, streakier and slightly darker version of the commoner Greenfinch. Males have a black cap and bib, a yellowish green breast and streaky black and green upperparts. Females have a much more subdued plumage, with less black on the head. Juveniles are brown and streaky.

## Behaviour
Often seen in flocks, and especially keen on seed and nut feeders in gardens. Conifers also help attract this species, and may even persuade them to nest. In early spring some male Siskins may start to sing in gardens, even though these birds will then head much farther north to breed in Scotland or Scandinavia.

FINCHES

Adult male

Adult female

Juvenile

## Breeding

Breeds mainly away from gardens in
conifer plantations and mixed
woodlands. Lays 3-6 pale bluish white
eggs, incubated for 11-14 days. Young
fledge after 13-15 days. Two broods.

Adult
female

## When & where

Resident throughout the year, though often
commoner in gardens in late autumn, winter and
especially early spring, when males may even begin
to sing during sunny weather. Fairly widespread
throughout Britain and Ireland in autumn and
winter, though during the breeding season ore
common in the west and north.

FINCHES

| J | F | M | A | M | J |
|---|---|---|---|---|---|
| J | A | S | O | N | D |

## ID FACT FILE

**SIZE**
Length 13.5cm
(5.25in). Smaller
than Greenfinch,
larger than
Goldfinch.

**LOOKALIKES**
Outside breeding
season can be
confused with
various small
brown birds.

**VOICE**
The Linnet's
song is a
delightful,
melodious series
of twitters and
whistles. Call a
soft twitter, often
uttered in flight
as it passes
overhead.

**FEEDING**
Feeds mainly on
insects during the
spring and
summer, while
outside these
seasons changes
to a diet of seeds.

# Linnet
*Carduelis cannabina*

Once a common bird of farmland and heathland areas, and taken for granted by many birdwatchers, the Linnet has undergone a major decline in the past few decades. This is almost certainly a result of the lack of seeds available on farmland in winter, because of the change towards planting arable crops all year round, and the general 'tidiness' of modern farming methods which allow little or no waste to remain in the fields. Linnets may still be seen in some gardens, however, especially those near fields – and may even come to feeders. Like Goldfinches, Linnets used to be kept widely as cage-birds for their song.

## Appearance
A small, neat finch, which in autumn and winter appears mainly buffish-brown with paler flashes on the wings in flight. During the breeding season, however, the male adopts a stunning rose-pink hue to his forehead and breast.

## Behaviour
Outside the breeding season Linnets travel in pairs, family parties or small flocks in search of food, and may cover a wide area. During the breeding season the male often perches on prominent song posts, such as gorse bushes, to deliver his delightful and charming song.

FINCHES

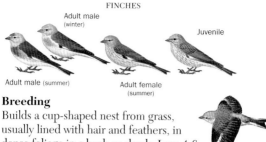

Adult male
(winter)

Juvenile

Adult male (summer)

Adult female
(summer)

## Breeding

Builds a cup-shaped nest from grass,
usually lined with hair and feathers, in
dense foliage in a bush or shrub. Lays 4-6
pale eggs, overlaid with faint marks which
look like pencil scribbles! They are
incubated for 10-14 days, and young fledge after
11-13 days. Two, sometimes three, broods.

Adult
female
(summer)

## When & where

Despite its rapid decline, the Linnet is still fairly
widespread in suitable lowland farming and heath
habitat in England and Wales, and also found in parts
of lowland Scotland and Ireland. Currently decreasing
rapidly, and like other farmland birds requires a
change in policy before this can be reversed.

| J | F | M | A | M | J |
|---|---|---|---|---|---|
| J | A | S | O | N | D |

## ID FACT FILE

**SIZE**
Length 12cm
(4.75in). Size of
Blue Tit.

**LOOKALIKES**
Similar to Linnet;
may also be
mistaken for
Siskin if not seen
well.

**VOICE**
Song a selection
of rapid,
staccato notes
like typewriter
keys; also gives
a range of trills
and whistling
calls, often in
flight.

**FEEDING**
Feeds mainly on
seeds and
insects, and will
occasionally
come to seed
feeders in
gardens.

# Lesser Redpoll
*Carduelis cabaret*

The taxonomy of this little finch is highly
complex, but the 'lesser' form was
recently 'split' from several other races of
Redpoll found in northern and western
Europe, and accorded a new status as a
full species. Unfortunately the Lesser
Redpoll has undergone a rapid decline
recently, like the Linnet and other seed-
eating birds; this is mainly due to a
change in farming methods which means
there are far fewer seeds available for the
birds during the autumn and winter
months.

### Appearance
A small, streaky finch; appearing mainly
buffish-brown, with darker back and
wings. Adults always show the crimson
patch on the forehead that gives the
species its name, and this is particularly
prominent in males during the breeding
season. During the spring and summer
months, when they are breeding, males
also have a pink breast. This may still
show, though less brightly, in autumn
and winter. Juveniles appear fairly
nondescript: brown and streaky.

### Behaviour
A sociable bird, almost always seen in
large flocks, which flit through the tops
of trees – especially alders near water. It
is often seen in the company of Siskins,
though unlike that species appears to be

FINCHES

Adult male (summer)  Adult male (winter)  Adult female (summer)  Juvenile

Adult female (summer)

less able to adapt to feeding in gardens. In winter it prefers wooded areas near running water where insects are likely to be more numerous.

## Breeding
Breeds mainly in birch and alder woodlands and on heathland, away from gardens. Lays 4-5 pale blue eggs with darker markings, incubated for 10-14 days. Young fledge after 11-14 days. One or two broods.

## When & where
Breeding strongholds are mainly in northern and western Britain; but the species is also found in parts of Ireland. In autumn and winter Redpolls are more widely spread, though are never very common. Numbers are currently decreasing rapidly.

| J | F | M | A | M | J |
|---|---|---|---|---|---|
| J | A | S | O | N | D |

# Bullfinch
*Pyrrhula pyrrhula*

## ID FACT FILE

**SIZE**
Length 14.5cm
(5.75in). Slightly
larger and bulkier
than House
Sparrow.

**LOOKALIKES**
Female can
resemble female
Chaffinch; male
unmistakable!

**VOICE**
A gentle, piping
'piu'. Song an
extended version
of this, with
additional
wheezing and
piping notes.

**FEEDING**
Feeds mainly on
seeds, crushed
in its large bill.
Also enjoys buds
of fruit trees,
making it an
agricultural pest
in some areas.

Once a common sight along our country hedgerows, this stunning finch has, along with other seed-eating birds, suffered a rapid and severe decline in numbers in recent years. This is almost certainly caused by a lack of food and nesting habitat available in autumn and winter, due to modern farming methods. Bullfinches are also a major agricultural pest, especially in areas with fruit orchards such as Kent, because of their habit of eating the buds of fruit trees.

## Appearance
Seen well, the male Bullfinch is quite simply unmistakable: with his black cap, grey back and bright cherry-pink throat, belly and breast. The female is a monochrome version of the male, being brownish below, but with the same black markings on the head and body. In flight both sexes show a distinctive white rump, which is especially obvious as they fly away from you!

## Behaviour
A shy species, easily flushed when alarmed, so it is not as easy to get good views of as many other members of the finch family. The Bullfinch tends to sit and feed quietly in a bush or hedgerow, so it is often best located by its call: a soft 'piu'.

FINCHES

Adult male    Adult female

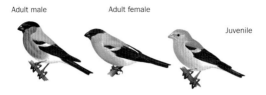

Juvenile

## Breeding
Builds its nest deep inside a bush or the foliage of a tree, making a loose cup from small twigs lined with hair and grass. Lays 3-6 pale blue eggs with fine black spots, incubated for 12-14 days. Young fledge after 15-17 days. Two, sometimes three, broods.

Adult female

## When & where
Resident but now scarce across much of its former range, though still found throughout most of Britain and Ireland apart from the extreme north and west.

| J | F | M | A | M | J |
|---|---|---|---|---|---|
| J | A | S | O | N | D |

### ID FACT FILE

**SIZE**
Length 18cm (7in). Our largest finch; almost size of Starling.

**LOOKALIKES**
Seen well, unmistakable; but could resemble female Bullfinch on poor views.

**VOICE**
Best located by its very loud flight call: an explosive 'zik'.

**FEEDING**
Feeds mainly on seeds and berries, such as cherries and beech nuts, which it crushes using its enormous and powerful bill.

# Hawfinch
*Coccothraustes coccothraustes*

Britain's largest species of finch is a magnificent bird, with a thick, heavy bill capable of exerting enormous pressure of several tons per square inch! This enables the birds to crush their favourite food of cherry stones. Hawfinches are amongst our shyest species, and as a result are rarely seen by birdwatchers. Your best bet is to locate a woodland where they roost in late afternoon during the autumn and winter, and listen for their distinctive call.

## Appearance
Rarely seen well, but when good views are obtained the Hawfinch is almost impossible to confuse with any other species. It is larger and even more thick-set and bull-necked in appearance than the Bullfinch, and much larger, more stocky and more orange or rust coloured than the male Chaffinch. The adult male has a rusty-orange head and underparts, a grey patch around the neck, and a dark back. The female is duller, though with similar plumage features. In flight it shows a prominent black and white wing pattern. Juveniles are very similar to their parents, though they lack the distinctive black throat.

## Behaviour
Very shy and unobtrusive, often hiding deep within the foliage of mature trees –

FINCHES

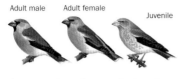

Adult male    Adult female

Juvenile

Adult female

with a special preference for hornbeam. It will occasionally visit gardens to feed, especially in rural areas near large areas of mature, broad-leaved woodland.

### Breeding
Builds a cup-shaped nest from small twigs lined with hair or grass, usually in dense foliage in woodland, where it lays 4-5 pale bluish white eggs with dark spots, incubated for 11-13 days. Young fledge after 10-14 days. One brood.

### When & where
Found in mature woodlands with beech or hornbeam in southern England and parts of East Anglia; also a few north to the Scottish borders. It is rare in Wales and absent from Ireland. Resident but currently in decline.

BUNTINGS

| J | F | M | A | M | J |
| J | A | S | O | N | D |

## ID FACT FILE

**SIZE**
Length 16.5cm (6.5in). Larger and longer-tailed than House Sparrow.

**LOOKALIKES**
Females can look superficially like other female buntings; males unmistakable.

**VOICE**
Song unmistakable: the famous 'a little bit of bread and no cheeeese'!

**FEEDING**
Feeds mainly on seeds and berries in winter, though switches to insects in spring and summer. Will occasionally visit artificial seed feeders in gardens.

# Yellowhammer
*Emberiza citrinella*

This stunning member of the bunting family has, along with so many other seed-eating species dependent on farmland, suffered extreme declines in the past fifty years or so. Nevertheless it can still be encountered in many rural areas, as it sings its well-known song. Its unusual name derives from an old German source, in which 'ammer' simply means 'little bird', and has nothing to do with the sound made by the species!

## Appearance
The breeding male is unmistakable: our only bright-yellow bird apart from the two species of wagtail, from which it differs considerably in shape and habits. The male has a bright-yellow head, face and underparts, which contrast with streaked, brownish upperparts. Winter males and females are much duller brown with yellowish streaks in the plumage. In flight it reveals a plain, unstreaked chestnut rump.

## Behaviour
A familiar bird of farmland fields and hedgerows, especially where there are plenty of weed seeds to feed on in autumn and winter. It is often seen perched on the top twig of a hedgerow, from which males deliver their characteristic song. The Yellowhammer breeds quite late in the season,

BUNTINGS

Adult male (summer)  Adult female (winter)  Adult female (summer)  Juvenile

Adult female (summer)

sometimes with young still in the nest in July and August, so males can often be heard singing well into late summer.

### Breeding

Builds a substantial nest out of grass or moss in a hedge or bank, or on the ground, where it lays 3-5 pale eggs with darker spots, incubated for 11-14 days. Young fledge after 12-13 days. Two or three broods.

### When & where

Following a major population crash, now widely but very thinly distributed across England, Wales and lowland Scotland. Scarce but widely found in Ireland. Currently undergoing major decline, which may be reversed by recent changes in farming policy.

| J | F | M | A | M | J |
|---|---|---|---|---|---|
| J | A | S | O | N | D |

## ID FACT FILE

**Size**
Length 15cm
(6in). Slightly
larger than
House Sparrow.

**Lookalikes**
Male in breeding
plumage
unmistakable;
female
superficially like
female House
Sparrow.

**Voice**
A monotonous,
flatly toned call
and song,
consisting of the
same note
repeated at brief
intervals, in a
hesitant and
rather bored
manner!

**Feeding**
Feeds mainly on
seeds, though
will also take
insects in
breeding season.

# Reed Bunting
*Emberiza schoeniclus*

Superficially resembling a House Sparrow, this attractive little bunting has undergone a major and widespread decline in recent years, along with many other farmland species. This is almost entirely due to due to food shortages on farmland caused by modern farming methods, but this may be halted by more sympathetic management of farming areas. However, at the same time it has taken to visiting gardens on a more regular basis than before, so paradoxically it may now be easier to see. In the breeding season it lives up to its name, usually nesting near large reedbeds where it can feed.

## Appearance
The male is very distinctive, with his smart black head, face and bib, and a thin grey line dividing the bib from the rest of his face. He also has brown, streaky upperparts and pale, greyish-white underparts, providing a contrasting appearance. Females, and males during the autumn and winter seasons, are less obvious, but have a subtle yet distinctive face pattern which distinguishes them from other buntings, sparrows and finches.

## Behaviour
Like most finches and buntings it prefers to feed in large flocks in autumn and winter, often in the company of other species. In the breeding season it is

BUNTINGS

Adult male (summer)  Adult male (winter)  Adult female (summer)  Juvenile

Adult female (summer)

usually found near water, with males perched on crops, reeds or small bushes to deliver their characteristically monotonous song.

## Breeding

Breeds mainly in farm crops (such as oil seed rape) or reed beds, laying 4-5 olive-coloured eggs with darker spots and blotches, incubated for 12-14 days. Young fledge after 10-13 days. Two, occasionally three, broods. Like other buntings, the Reed Bunting tends to nest quite late into the summer season, so its nests may be vulnerable to being destroyed if they are in harvest crops.

## When & where

Widely if sometimes thinly distributed across England, Wales, lowland Scotland and Ireland where it is resident.

# SPECIES INDEX

*Accipiter nisus* 32, 33, 34, 74-75
*Aegithalos caudatus* 14, 180-181
*Aix galericulata* 70-71
*Alauda arvensis* 124-125
*Alcedo atthis* 38, 112-113
*Alopochen aegyptiacus* 54-55
*Anas clypeata* 37, 58-59
*Anas penelope* 60-61
*Anas platyrhynchos* 5, 56-57
*Anas strepera* 62-63
*Anas crecca* 64-65
*Anthus pratensis* 134-135
*Apus apus* 110-111
*Ardea cinerea* 46-47
*Aythya ferina* 37, 68-69
*Aythya fuligula* 5, 37, 66-67

Blackbird 8, 14, 18, 154-155
Blackcap 8, 11, 14, 20, 38, 168-169
*Bombycilla garrulus* 142-143
Brambling 214-215
*Branta canadensis* 52-53
Bullfinch 19, 228-229
Bunting, Reed 234-235

*Carduelis cabaret* 19, 226-227
*Carduelis cannabina* 224-225
*Carduelis carduelis* 8, 14, 220-221
*Carduelis chloris* 13, 21, 23, 218-219
*Carduelis spinus* 8, 19, 222-223
*Certhia brachydactyla* 194-195
*Certhia familiaris* 24, 38, 192-193
Chaffinch 212-213
Chiffchaff 38, 170-171
*Ciconia ciconia* 9, 48-49
*Coccothraustes coccothraustes* 230-231

*Columba livia* 98-99
*Columba oenas* 100-101
*Columba palumbus* 14, 102-103
Coot 37, 84-85
Cormorant 44-45
*Corvus cornix* 206-207
*Corvus corone* 204-205
*Corvus monedula* 202-203
Crow, Carrion 204-205
Crow, Hooded 206-207
*Cygnus olor* 50

*Delichon urbica* 9, 24, 132-133
*Dendrocopos major* 120-121
*Dendrocopus minor* 122-123
Dove, Collared 14, 21, 104-105
Dove, Stock 100-101
Duck, Tufted 5, 37, 66-67
Duck, Mandarin 70-71
Duck, Ruddy 72-73
Dunnock 18, 38, 146-147

*Emberiza citrinella* 232-233
*Emberiza schoeniclus* 234-235
*Erithacus rubecula* 8, 14, 18, 24, 38, 148-149

*Falco peregrinus* 76-77
*Falco subbuteo* 78-79
*Falco tinnunculus* 24, 80-81
Fieldfare 11, 21, 156-157
Firecrest 176-177
Flycatcher, Spotted 24, 178-9
*Fringilla coelebs* 212-213
*Fringilla montifringilla* 214-215
*Fulica atra* 37, 84-85

Gadwall 62-63
*Galerida cristata* 126-127
*Gallinula chloropus* 37, 86-87
*Garrulus glandarius* 14, 33, 37, 198-199

Goldcrest 21, 174-175
Goldfinch 8, 14, 220-221
Goose, Canada 52-53
Goose, Egyptian 54-55
Grebe, Great Crested 37, 40-41
Grebe, Little 37, 42-43
Greenfinch 13, 21, 23, 218-219
Gull, Black-headed 88-89
Gull, Common 90-91
Gull, Herring 37, 92-93
Gull, Lesser Black-backed
    37, 94-95

Hawfinch 230-231
Heron, Grey 46-47
Hirundo rustica 9, 130-131
Hobby 78-79
Hoopoe 114-115

Jay 14, 33, 37, 198-199
Jackdaw 202-203
Jynx torquilla 116-117

Kestrel 24, 80-81
Kingfisher 38, 112-113

Lark, Crested 126-127
Larus argentatus 36, 92-93
Larus fuscus 36, 94-95
Larus canus 90-91
Larus ridibundus 88-89
Linnet 224-225
Luscinia megarhynchos
    150-151

Magpie 32, 33, 36, 200-201
Mallard 5, 56-57
Martin, House 9, 24, 132-133
Martin, Sand 128-129
Moorhen 37, 86-87
Motacilla alba 24, 140-141
Motacilla cinerea 138-139
Motacilla flava 136-137
Muscicapa striata 24, 178-9

Nightingale 150-151
Nuthatch 38, 190-191

Oriole, Golden 9, 196-197
Oriolus oriolus 9, 196-197
Owl, Barn 24
Owl, Tawny 108-109
Oxyura jamaicensis 72-73

Parakeet, Ring-necked 106-107
Parus ater 184-185
Parus caeruleus 5, 8, 11, 13, 24,
    24, 186-187
Parus major 11, 13, 24,
    188-189
Parus palustris 182-183
Passer domesticus 5, 7, 13, 14,
    21, 22, 23, 24, 210-211
Peregrine 76-77
Phalacrocorax carbo 44-45
Phasianus colchicus 82-83
Pheasant 82-83
Phoenicurus ochruros 152-153
Phylloscopus collybita 38,
    170-171
Phylloscopus trochilus 38,
    172-173
Pica pica 32, 33, 36, 200-201
Picus viridis 37, 118-119
Pigeon, Feral 98-99
Pigeon, Wood 14, 102-103
Pipit, Meadow 134-135
Pochard 37, 68-69
Podiceps cristatus 37, 40-41
Prunella modularis 18, 38,
    146-147
Psittacula krameri 106-107
Pyrrhula pyrrhula 21, 228-229

Redpoll, Lesser 19, 226-227
Redstart, Black 152-153
Redwing 11, 21, 160-161
Regulus ignicapillus 176-177
Regulus regulus 21, 174-175

*Riparia riparia* 128-129
Robin 8, 14, 18, 24, 38,
    148-149

Serin 9, 216-217
*Serinus serinus* 9, 216-217
Shoveler 37, 58-59
*Sitta europaea* 38, 190-191
Skylark 124-125
Siskin 8, 19, 222-223
Sparrow, House 5, 7, 13,
    14, 21, 22, 23, 24, 210-211
Sparrowhawk 32, 33, 34,
    180-181
Starling 7, 22, 208-209
*Sterna hirundo* 96-97
Stork, White 9, 48-49
*Streptopelia decaocto* 14, 21,
    104-105
*Strix aluco* 108-109
*Sturnus vulgaris* 7, 22, 208-209
Swallow 9, 130-131
Swan, Mute 50
Swift 110-111
*Sylvia atricapilla* 8, 11, 14, 20,
    38, 168-169
*Sylvia borin* 166-167
*Sylvia communis* 20, 38,
    164-165

*Tachybaptus ruficollis* 37,
    42-43
Teal 64-65
Tern, Common 96-97
Thrush, Mistle 18, 21, 38,
    162-163
Thrush, Song 7, 18, 22, 34,
    158-159
Tit, Blue 5, 8, 11, 13, 24,
    186-187
Tit, Coal 184-185
Tit, Great 11, 13, 24, 188-189
Tit, Long-tailed 14, 180
Tit, Marsh 182-183

Treecreeper 24, 38, 192-193
Treecreeper, Short-toed
    194-195
*Troglodytes troglodytes* 8, 18,
    20, 23, 38, 144-145
*Turdus iliacus* 11, 21, 160-161
*Turdus merula* 8, 14, 18,
    154-155
*Turdus philomelos* 7, 18, 22,
    34, 158-159
*Turdus pilaris* 11, 21, 156-157
*Turdus viscivorus* 18, 21, 38,
    162-163
*Tyto alba* 24

*Upupa epops* 114-115

Wagtail, Grey 138-139
Wagtail, Pied/White 24,
    140-141
Wagtail, Yellow 136-137
Warbler, Garden 166-167
Warbler, Willow 38, 172-173
Waxwing 142-143
Whitethroat 20, 38, 164-165
Wigeon 60-61
Woodpecker, Great Spotted
    120-121
Woodpecker, Green 37,
    118-119
Woodpecker, Lesser Spotted
    122-123
Wren 8, 18, 20, 23, 38,
    144-145
Wryneck 116-117

Yellowhammer 232-233

# UBJECT INDEX

lder 19
pple 18, 19

aby birds, care of 27
erberis 23
ig Garden BirdWatch 16
inoculars 8
ird baths 29
ird tables 12, 14, 16
ramble 18, 20
rown Rat 32
TO (British Trust for
rnithology) 16, 25, 26
uddleia 19

ats 15, 26, 32-34
lematis 17, 23
ornflower 20
otoneaster 18, 21
owslip 20
rab apple 19

lder 20, 23

eeding & feeders 10-16
orsythia 21

rey Squirrel 32

awthorn 20, 23
olly 18
oneysuckle 17, 20, 23

vy 17, 20, 23

ive food 14
eylandii cypress 21, 23

Nesting & nestboxes 22-27
Nyger seed 14

Oak 18

Pests 32-34
Peanuts 13
Planting for birds 17-21
Plants
berry-bearing 17, 18
climbing 17, 22-23
flowering 17
native 19
non-native 19, 21
seed-bearing 17
Ponds 30-31
Poppy 20
Predators 32-34
Pyracantha 21

RSPB (Royal Society for
the Protection of Birds) 16,
21, 25

Stinging nettle 20
Sunflower 17, 21
Sunflower seed 13

Teasel 17
Towns & parks 36-39

Water 28-31, 35
Willow 19
Wood Mouse 32

# ● Collins

If you have enjoyed this book, why not have a look at
some of the other titles in the WILD GUIDE series?